CW00523771

Producer & International Distributor
eBookPro Publishing
www.ebook-pro.com

Super-Exercise Training:
Dr. Michael Herling

Translation: Yonatan Boxman

Website: https://superexercises.com/

Contact: mickyhe@yahoo.com
ISBN 9798800003765

SUPER-EXERCISE
TRAINING

A FAMILY DOCTOR'S ULTIMATE SYSTEM
TO ACHIEVING EXCELLENT LIFELONG FITNESS

DR. MICHAEL HERLING

Contents

INTRODUCTION

We all want to be healthy, happy and strong throughout our lives. At the same time, we are all aware of the obstacles that stand in the way of realizing this desire. Life is a long and challenging journey. We all know that being fit physically (and mentally) can tremendously help and support us throughout this journey. Nonetheless, "being fit" proves to be an elusive concept. Most people get it completely wrong. Regardless of whether they get it wrong by over-moving, under-moving or not moving, injuries and slow, age-associated physical deterioration are the result. I was trained as a family physician to encourage patients to be physically active. Physical activity is part of a healthy lifestyle. So, for many years I would tell my patients how important it was for them to work out and be fit. Like many doctors, I told my patients to go to the gym or to choose an active hobby they like and to just do it. Most of my patients nodded and continued to under-move. Compliance was nearly nonexistent.

I felt I needed a different approach. Maybe I was to blame for this low compliance and not the "lazy and uninformed" patients. I started asking myself all kinds of new questions. Like what was our body designed to do when it developed into its more-or-less current shape millions of years ago? What is the precise movement dosage required for the average person to achieve proper fitness? What is proper fitness? Can I invent a new fitness system out of thin air? Can excellent fitness be preserved throughout our entire lives and even improved? Can I design a fitness system that anyone can perform? At any age? At any fitness level? Even patients with serious health issues? Why do so many people fail to move themselves properly? How can I jumpstart an unmotivated patient into proper movement in a few minutes? What is the secret of older athletes who enjoy excellent fitness even in their seventies and eighties? What are the best exercises in the world?

In the following pages you will learn about the answers and solutions I reached. The system I designed has the power, as you will soon see, to revolutionize the way we approach movement and fitness. For the last six years I have had the pleasure of sharing my insights with thousands of patients, therapists, (especially physiotherapists, psychologists, and family doctors) trainers and athletes.

To design a new system from the ground up is far from easy. I had to deconstruct every element and variable movement is composed of, and then reconstruct it into something that was both innovative and applicable. I named my new system "Super-Exercise Training" or SET. This journey evolved into a prolonged process of experimentation, discovery, questioning, trial and error: What works? What doesn't? My background as a holistic family doctor deeply influenced the result. Physical activity is not just a bunch of exercises done twice a week but rather a complex tool that can assist us in being as healthy, strong and happy as possible. Viewing human movement from a bird's eye perspective, I immediately saw the need to incorporate several elements in the system that are often neglected in the established exercise methodologies; anti-aging exercises for instance, exercises for specific diseases, healthy breathing, and a special focus on our connective tissue, as well as other neglected areas.

Super-exercise training is all about optimization. Finding the way to slowly develop excellent fitness through daily simple, short, easy, safe, intuitive and wise movement. By implementing the principles of

SET, proper fitness is guaranteed. Why am I so certain? Because every animal in nature is performing SET daily, and they effortlessly achieve, well, animalistic fitness. Every child in the world moves according to SET principles and is effortlessly fit and agile. All the extremely fit elderly people I met intuitively move according to SET principles. Last but not least, anyone who has managed to embed the system in their daily life, whether as a result of being my patient, reading this book, hearing a lecture or having participated in a workshop, witnessed an effortless improvement in their fitness level.

At the age of 55, I enjoy - knock on wood - the best fitness level of my life. I skateboard in parks on a weekly basis. (My best tricks are boardslide on a rail, 5-0 frontside grind and four stairs ollie.) I surf on a short board and on a devilishly short paddleboard, I windsurf and snowboard and do a lot of fun bodyweight exercises like front levers, muscle ups and even managed to be the oldest participant to pass the preliminaries for the semifinals of Israel's "Ninja Warrior," a reality television show. I use my own system daily to support my hobbies and enjoy a pain and injury-free life. I do so despite severe time constraints. I have a busy clinic to run, I lecture a lot, I write a blog, I record a podcast, all this while raising four kids (the oldest of whom is 17 years old and the youngest is 4 years old) and I must also read daily, mostly professional material, as I'm a compulsive reader. I also must play some musical instrument daily. This does not leave much time for movement so I have no choice but to optimize the few minutes I have every day to keep myself fit.

SET is designed specifically to be a lifelong practice. Somehow, regardless of the system we are currently practicing, it is almost guaranteed that we will drop out. Not so with SET. SET gives everyone the immediate opportunity to adopt a comprehensive movement system for life. It requires no trainer, almost no time investment, it can be done anywhere and is simple enough for just about anyone to hop on the bandwagon. And once you understand and internalize the principles, I'm afraid there is no turning back. You deeply recognize that this is the way to go about moving. The principles and premises of SET can be used to enhance and cultivate anybody's fitness. And although we tend to think that movement is all about great muscle strength and cardiovascular capacity, movement is actually all about the brain. The brain orchestrates everything: decision making, motivation, mental endurance, learning new skills, intelligence, coordination, posture, coping with stress, setting priorities. All these things happen before we lift a finger and are addressed before and as we move. That is why in SET, your brain will be fully engaged. Unlike other systems, there is no trainer instructing you when, how, and for how long to move and there are no predetermined programs. You are your own trainer. You fully own your own movement. You determine all the parameters of the training session. The duration, the types of exercises, their intensity, the variations, the time of day, etc. By becoming your own trainer, equipped with the knowledge and tools in this book, you will be able to easily and intuitively tap into your own potential, and slowly and safely cultivate your fitness throughout your entire life.

SET has a theoretical and a philosophical side. It is my intention to enrich your understanding of movement and use this knowledge to motivate and direct you to a wiser and more optimized movement.

As I write this introduction, many people have already understood and internalized the system. They have become the masters of their own bodies and movement, and have gained experience in the benefits of a movement method that is more playful, creative, intuitive, and in tune with their life.

Unlike most other workout systems, SET is fully compatible with any other exercise system. I do not oppose any such systems since active movement is always positive. Moreover, you can apply SET's principles to any activity or sportive hobby.

In the first chapter, I analyze all the variables of movement — the environment, animalistic movement characteristics, the components of physical movement, the trainee, the trainer, the dosage, the training period and the breathing.

In the second chapter, I lay down the philosophy and the principles behind the super-exercise training model.

The third chapter presents specific super-exercises and how to perform them.

The fourth chapter describes the best exercises for cultivating each component of movement.

In the fifth chapter, I analyze movement throughout the life cycle as it changes from our first years onward.

In the sixth chapter, I share my clinical experience on how SET can aid in treating diverse health complications.

Chapter Seven is all about the critical importance of our connective tissue (fascia).

In Chapter Eight, I expand on the mental aspect of moving.

Chapter Nine discusses the relevance of SET to the amateur athlete.

And finally, Chapter Ten discusses the dangers of a sedentary lifestyle.

So, it's time to roll up our sleeves and dive into the fascinating and playful world of human movement

Enjoy the ride,
Dr. Herling

CHAPTER 1

The Pattern of Physical Activity

To construct an optimal model of physical activity — a model that will enable us to maintain our fitness throughout our life cycle and even improve it, and that will make us want to move our body at any age — we must first understand, in depth, the components of physical movement as well as the unique characteristics of every component. In this first chapter of the book, we will therefore consider the fascinating array of human movement and examine each distinctive characteristic: the environment, the components of the movement, the trainee, the trainer, the dosage, the time and the breathing. The model of the super-exercises training that I developed is based on taking all of these variables into account, with their use being flexible and subject to change, in order to enable diverse, spontaneous, and dynamically changing activity — activity which can be easily performed anywhere and anytime.

1.1 FIRST VARIABLE – THE MOTION ENVIRONMENT: FROM ENVIRONMENTAL DIVERSITY TO MOTION BLOCKS

The human body is characterized by incredible motoric complexity, enabling it to generate millions of motion combinations. Our ever-so-elegant muscle motions enable us to play the piano and assemble complex tools. Throughout history, countless movement methods have been developed. But why? Why are our bodies' motions so diverse? Why do we possess such an incredible repertoire of motion options?

Simple observation of the natural world makes clear that the human body was designed to move and operate in three distinct ecological/ geographical environments, utilizing a different array of movements in each:

- The ground environment – our body can walk, run, crawl, roll, lift weights, drag weights, push and hunt on the surface.
- The water environment – our body was also designed to swim, and more importantly to hold its breath and dive, and even to hunt in an aqueous environment.
- Climbing – our body is apelike, resembling the primordial ancestors from whom we inherited the ability to grip with our hands and, to some extent, with our feet as well.

In each of the three environments, the human body utilizes completely different capabilities. Three completely different neuromuscular systems, each meaningful only in its own specific environment, are embedded in a single biological system. Swimming and diving motions are utterly meaningless on the ground or amidst the canopies of trees. By the same measure, walking serves no purpose in the water or amongst the branches, and climbing is utterly superfluous on the ground or in the water. The combination of these three capabilities is unique to human beings. No other mammal on earth can move and hunt so efficiency in these three environments. This impressive environmental versatility is only possible thanks to our body's unique joints and muscles (e.g., shoulders, hips and palms). The range of motions and body stances we are capable of assuming and exploiting to move through space is nearly infinite. This versatility provided our ancestors with a considerable evolutionary advantage as it improved their chances to hunt and gather food in each of the three environments, particularly from the seas and lakes. More food meant more protein and more fish fat. According to one theory, the ability to access the food sources in rivers, lakes and seas was one of the reasons for the turning point in the evolution of our hominid ancestors into upright primates with larger brains, and the continued development into a human sized brain. The study of human brain development is extremely controversial, but it is nonetheless undisputed that a larger brain allows for greater motor control and can produce more refined motions. Via feedback, more refined movements also influence brain and muscle development, resulting in more refined muscles, such as those in the face and the palms, enabling us to play the piano or perform a complex choreographic dance.

However, in the modern era, the fitness industry has invented a new environment for physical activity. The ground, water and trees were joined by the box/block. Or to be more exact – four types of boxes in which our movements occur.

- **Time boxes**

It starts with the 13:00 to 14:00 physical education class in schools where children exercise 3 times a week for 30-60 minutes. It continues with "adult" physical activities we define as "fitness" or "physical training" or "hobbies." We clear a block of time – usually an hour, several times a week for this activity. In contrast, movement in nature flows of its own volition, in accordance with the environmental conditions or the needs of the animal, until it eventually ends – once again, subject to the environmental conditions or the needs of the animal. Time in and of itself is meaningless. Time is an artificial block invented to frame our activity, forcing us to move according to a predefined schedule, and for predefined intervals of time. The problem with this idea is that it leads many individuals to completely avoid any form of physical activity, because they lack the time, willpower or energy to commit to such prolonged intervals of time.

Since one of the common myths of the fitness industry is that physical activity must be performed often, the prospective trainees commit themselves to begin to carry out physical activity, but soon give up and quit. Consistent persistence in performing the physical activity over such a long-time block requires us to be attracted to the activity we choose – even to love it. But what if pacing back and forth bores us? What if we aren't attracted to any sport? The idea that physical activity must take place in blocks of time is a concept that is imprisoning all of us. Each and every one of us, no exceptions, is convinced that we must sweat and exert ourselves during specific periods and over a prolonged period of time, or else the activity will be completely useless.

- **Structural blocks**

The activity occurring within time blocks is usually also performed within cubic, block-like structures that are also physically constructed out of block-like bricks: the gym, the pool, the basketball court, the yoga studio – all are built in straight lines and angles, just like the office, home and shopping mall where most of our movement takes place. These blocks cut us off from the chance to move in the dynamic exterior, natural environment. We identify and associate our physical activity with a block that is there – outside the home and the job, in a known address. In nature, that idea also does not exist. Animals move wherever they happen to be. They don't go somewhere in order to "exercise." A bird does not fly twice a week to the tree from which she conducts "flying workouts." Likewise, a cheetah does not march to a savannah where it conducts "running exercises."

- **Motion blocks**

Blocks of time spent exercising within structural blocks result in a straight, monotonous, and repetitive motion: walking or running, whether on a treadmill or the track, swimming laps, riding a bicycle, lifting weights, or any number of gym activities. Even less-linear activities that are practiced within the constraints of a block, such as in yoga, are repetitive and eventually lead most people to boredom and abandoning the activity. In nature, animals of course never move in straight lines and straight angels, and neither do children. Movement in a straight line is a modern invention, which flies in the face of our natural, spontaneous animalistic origins.

- **Mental blocks**

Any activity performed within the constraints of a time block, structural block and motion block eventually must also lead to a mental block and to a total suffocation of our intuition and physical instincts. Let us suppose, for example, that I am participating in a soccer practice, and my instinct tells me to pick up the ball with my hands. According to the strict rules of the game, I am of course forbidden from doing so. Should I touch the ball with my hand, I would be punished for this. The fitness industry comes up with endless regulations on movement – a variety of laws for Olympic sports, instructions for trainees such as "perform ten repetitions three times," and so on. Whenever I recommend a given exercise to trainees, the questions almost inevitably surface. "So how many times do I need to repeat the exercise? For how long? How many times a week?" Questions of this sort illustrate well the fact that our mind has long since lost touch with our body and the intuitive ability to act in accordance to its needs, and the way it was destined and engineered to move. A child does not ask how long to play and how many times he should climb up or descend from a tree. He simply does so until he has had enough. The mental block paralyzes our intuition and eventually leads most people to drop out from the world of movement.

Monotonous, straight line, time and structural block-limited motion performed out of a fixated approach is not more than a parody on how we are supposed to move. In my eyes, this is no less than a "sacrilege of motion."

Does this mean the blocks must be completely abandoned? Not necessarily. Movement within blocks occasionally, or for short periods, can certainly support a hobby we are passionate about.

However, the main purpose must be movement that is not time-limited and that takes place in nature or in a location where we are not subject to constant rules and instructions. It must be constantly varied and dynamic, with the parameters of movement being determined solely by our intuition and immediate environment.

In order to realize your physical potential, I recommend incorporating all three environments (earth, water and trees) in your daily or weekly motion menu – and also the entire array of motion associated with each environment. The hardest environment for most people to access is water, since most of us lack access to the sea or a pool, lake or river. At the very least, your daily motion must include, other than the ground environment, the tree environment with its array of climbing movements. That is why in the super-exercise training, the elements of apelike holding and hanging are always included.

1.2 SECOND VARIABLE – CHARACTERISTICS OF ANIMALIS-TIC MOVEMENT

Whenever I want to illustrate to my patients the principles of natural movement, I show them pictures of Papuans who still live as hunter gatherers in nature. These tribesmen have no type of sports and no fitness trainers, and yet they still look fit. Very fit – "animal fitness." Even though nowadays we usually don't need our animalism to secure food and survive (though soldiers, for example, undergo intensive "animalistic" training to develop their animalistic stamina to protect themselves and us), we only exist here and now thanks to the fact that our ancestors successfully survived in a completely different environment. They had to optimally utilize their body to hunt, fight and escape predators.

Our animalistic aspect is embedded deep in our genes and our neuronal wiring. The electrical impulses our nerve cells transmit, which in turn cause muscle contraction, define every advanced animal species. Therefore, the study of animal movement and understanding their characteristics is a good way of understanding human motion, and by implementing aspects of animalistic movement we can improve both our fitness and our health.

• **Every day, all day**

Animals constantly move. They don't have days off, vacations or sabbaticals. Animals do not move in prolonged blocks of time several times a week. They have no trainers to instruct them how much and how powerfully to move. Animals have no exercises. Animals simply move every day, all day, in accordance to their needs, their environment and their body structure.

- **For your entire life**

Parrots, elephants, giant turtles and whales enjoy a long lifespan that is equivalent to, and sometimes greater, than ours. If we simply observe a flock of flying parrots, a herd of elephants, a bale of turtles or a pod of whales, we will have a very hard time identifying the 80-year-old parrot, 65-year-old elephant, 90-year-old turtle, or 150-year old whale. These animals, and in fact all animals, move gracefully at any age. They never undergo motion retirement. Human beings, on the other hand, avoid movement at almost every age, if they only have the chance. Once we reach the third age (65-90), most of us completely stop moving our body.

- **Everywhere**

Animals are always in movement regardless of where they happen to be. This may seem obvious, and yet, modern day individuals limit movement to the gym, the swimming pool, the yoga studio, or the treadmill. The eagle spreads its wings and flies. It does not waddle to a cage, hook itself up to a flight simulator, and then hover in place while staring at a flat screen displaying eagles chatting with each other.

- **Every which way**

Since animals move in nature, they are influenced by constantly changing environmental conditions. A monkey, for example, moves slightly differently every time he climbs, for the trees he climbs are completely different than one another. The shape of the branch, too, its angle, its thickness, the extent of its moisture, and the distances between the branches also change. It is influenced by the location of fruit, potential enemies, the wanderings of the ape tribe, dynamic social interactions, the seasonally changing landscape and more. Animals never move in straight lines or in a set path.

- **Alertness**

Life in nature is never completely safe. It is always wrapped up in dangers – the danger of hunger, the danger from other predators, and quite often danger from animals of the same gender. The danger leads to animals' senses being on constant alert. They are always aware of what is going on around them and always prepared to take immediate action. Animals do not require any warmup before they take action.

- **All out**

In nature, animals "give their all" to secure food, to run, or to struggle with other animals. Danger serves as an optimal trigger for action as far as speed, precision and power are concerned. A street cat, for example, can frequently find himself fleeing as rapidly as he can from an approaching car, a threatening human, or another animal. These "all-out" situations usually only last for a few critical seconds, in which the success in capturing the prey or fleeing the predator is determined. All-out situations which last minutes, let alone hours, are extremely rare in nature (for example, rams battling each other for hours or days for reproduction access to a desirable female). For humans in the modern world, "all-out" situations are naturally rare in daily life. They can occur, for example, when we cross the street and a car accelerates toward us rapidly. However, practicing these "all-out" situations is extremely important to our health, and that is what the HIIT training – High Intensity Interval Training – is based upon. Modern research has shown that this training method is just as effective as classic cardiovascular training, and sometimes even more so. (See, for example,

Gillen et al., 2016 and the "The One-Minute Workout Designed by Scientists" by Dr. Martin Gible and Christopher Shulgen that deal with physiology and the health advantages of the HIIT training.)

- **Lean and Mean**

In nature, animals are always slim and always fit. An animal which moves in accordance to its gene pattern in the environment where this pattern was forged, will be slim and in excellent shape by definition.

1.3 THIRD VARIABLE – COMPONENTS OF PHYSICAL MOVEMENT

Physical movement is based on seven components which appear in different compositions depending on the nature of the motion: strength, speed, flexibility, balance, coordination, endurance and posture. Human movement encompasses all these components. Moshe Feldenkrais, the developer of the Feldenkrais method, was once asked what a correct movement was. His response was, "A movement which helps us survive." To survive in three different existential environments, humans required all of these movement components.

Unlike us, many animals do not require advanced coordination. Many animals are not flexible, and others, such as birds, are distinguished by high speed and endurance, but not strength.

Physical training should include all movement components, and will thereby be a varied training by definition. Only through varied training can one develop stable and wise muscles that can operate in a variety of situations and possibilities.

The coordinator of all the movement components is the brain. Most of us believe that excellent physical fitness is the result of strong and flexible muscles. However, the brain is behind each and every movement, whether slow or fast, strong or weak, stable or unbalanced. Just like a lackluster orchestra conductor can make even the best orchestra sound bad, whereas a gifted conductor can make even a mediocre band sound wonderful — so too can our brain transform physical movement into either mediocrity or a magnificent harmonic concert. Our brain is what synchronizes the various components and activities, and determines how many and which muscle units we will recruit to achieve the desired strength and speed.

Electrical movement in the brain is different in character from muscle movement, which is biomechanical in nature. In the past, the human brain had to synchronize the movements of the entire body during hunting, flight or combat in an unfamiliar environment. Today, however, it is exempt from these responsibilities. The physical activity we perform, such as running on the treadmill or weightlifting, does not require much "brain power," for this is a monotonous, automatic activity taking place in a sterile environment. Many of the injuries and pain we suffer from in our joints and muscles actually originate in the brain; the brain has a difficult time synchronizing stable movement, recruiting sufficient muscles units in real time, synchronizing the movement together with the balance keeping inner ear, and performing movements which require an exact sequence of events. That is one of the main problems underlying physical movement difficulties during the third age. Beyond the dwindling of bones and muscles, degeneration of the brain cells and reduced capacities of the brain takes place as well! In order to preserve our brain at peak condition throughout our life cycle, we must keep it involved in wise and precise movement – movement that immediately awakens the entire brain. That is how we can prevent, minimize and delay the deterioration of the brain, or "dementia" as it is called in medical jargon. Moreover, varied physical movement, based on the maximum number of components, can significantly improve general well-being, health and fitness even at an older age.

A patient case of mine illustrating this scenario is the 78-year-old Solomon (fictitious name). Solomon came to my clinic after falling down while he was walking, to show me the hematoma which developed in his hip and hand following the fall.

Solomon is an extremely active individual according to any criteria. He walks four times a week, two hours every time, and twice a week he exercises in a gym under the guidance of a personal trainer. Nonetheless, his movement repertoire lacks two critical components. The first is speed: Solomon no longer performs rapid movements with his body. So when he had to perform such a rapid movement, stretching his leg forward to prevent the fall, he could not do so.

The second component is that Solomon does not involve his brain in any way in the activities he performs. Monotonous walking over the course of two hours does not require much brain activity. In the gym as well, he merely automatically carries out the instructions of the trainer. The last time he performed an "all-out" activity was in a high school athletics contest. Like most individuals his age, he performs comfortable, sedate physical activity that never calls upon 150 percent of his capacities for a short period of time. I explained to Solomon that beyond the considerable time he invests in physical activity, it is imperative to involve his mind. He must also train with the speed component every day in order to prevent future falls, as much as possible, which can have dangerous repercussions in advanced ages. I showed him how he could easily perform all-out isometric exercises and vary his walk in many different ways. I demonstrated to him in the clinic how to do so, and he repeated the exercises after me, performed them and understood them. In my next meeting with him, he told me that he had begun to vary his walks, and that to his surprise he had begun to enjoy them. He also reported a better overall feeling, a feeling that he was more "fit."

1.4 FOURTH VARIABLE – THE TRAINEE

Each and every one of us has a unique pattern of physical movement which is influenced by many personal parameters. The type of work we do – physical or office work; the place we live – in the polar regions, the desert, or the heart of a major city; the extent of our knowledge about physical activity; the amount of free time we enjoy; our medical condition; any injuries we may have suffered; the quality of our sleep; our mood; how we deal with pressure and failure; the character and quality of our diet; our body type; our friends – all of these variables have profound influence on the nature of our motions.

Our personal goals are another important parameter. Is our goal to transform ourselves into professional athletes, or to become healthier as the doctor ordered, or perhaps to sit before the computer and make money? Since, in the present day and age, physical movement is an activity we must initiate, we need to have a goal and we must understand the benefit we derive from this initiative. Forming the parameter of personal goals is in fact a mental process that generates motivation and persistence via learning and understanding. "Quitters never win, and winners never quit," Napoleon Hill, the first American guru of motivation and self-fulfillment, once said. Unfortunately, experience shows us that most of us do choose to quit. Usually we only do what we must do and no more. A large proportion of people have abandoned movement completely. Most of us know that we must move our body and lose weight, but we lack the willpower, time, motivation and/or money. At some point, all training programs fail for most people. Regardless of how wonderful they are or how charismatic the trainer is, at some point we just stop performing them. Some people begin and stop performing physical activity in a sort of yoyo-like pattern, or hop from one method to another. Others engage in some physical activity, but only if it matches their schedule and does not force them to leave their comfort zone; for example, bicycle riding on Saturday. All of us have our own reasons and circumstances, but the bottom line is that if the goal we set for ourselves is a strong and supple body, then that goal requires motivation and persistence, at least in the first few months, until we form a habit. Habits can become second nature, especially if they are simple, short and practical – like brushing our teeth.

Persistence is the key variable as far as physical training is concerned. In fact, all that really needs to be taught in schools and in training is how to persist. **Persistence can only be taught via persistence**.

The super-exercise model was developed to bypass most of the personal variables. Your health conditions, income level goals or personal preferences have no importance in this model. Super-exercises are universal and, as you will see later, are easy to learn and to perform, and can be carried out at any place and any time. Thanks to their ease and simplicity, these exercises will rapidly become regular daily habits.

1.5 FIFTH VARIABLE – THE TRAINING

All of us have some experience in some sort of training – it may be PE class, soccer, running, basketball, or perhaps martial arts training. Today, hundreds, and even thousands of training methods are available for those who seek them; ranging from the simplest such as walking or running, to traditional Far Eastern arts such as yoga and tai chi, martial arts and dancing, alongside such modern methods such as weightlifting and bodybuilding, plyometrics, CrossFit, Feldenkrais and the Alexander Technique, and even including Olympic sports, acrobatics and more. Each of these methods has numerous personal varieties developed by trainers throughout the world. This dizzying variety represents the infinite variety of human movement. Each of these methods and forms of physical activity has a unique motion components profile. Long distance running, for example, calls upon much endurance, but little power, balance and posture, and zero co-ordination, flexibility and speed.

Which training method should you choose? Each method has its own advantages and disadvantages. Some of these methods are very difficult and are destined to result in injuries or accelerated joint erosion. For example, choosing long distance running may, over time, lead to erosion of the joints and pain particularly in the third age. Other sports, such as American football or white-water kayaking, may even lead to severe injuries. Some training methods will simply bore you and lead you to abandon the activity, whereas others require a stiff and precise training schedule that makes persistence difficult, and which will likewise lead to abandonment. Some methods will lead your body to specialize in one particular component, but at the expense of others (for example, a very muscular but inflexible body). Some only address fitness at certain ages, whereas others are excellent but are not suitable to your physical condition, lifestyle, or busy schedule. That is why, when you choose the training method, it is important to carefully consider its unique aspects and primarily consider its safety, and the extent to which it addresses all movement components.

Beyond selecting a preferred method, there is also the issue of the training format. Most people associate training with physical activity that must be performed in extended time blocks – at least an hour, several time a weak, within structural blocks to which one must usually drive, or else commit to extended walks and runs.

However, the very thought of training over an extended time block constitutes a tremendous obstacle for many people who might want to "train," but cannot find the strength, time or money to do so. Between a vague desire of most of us to train, and an inflexible and high-commitment training format, there is a wide chasm which many fail to cross to reach their goal of exercise. Most of us have experienced it personally. We begin training in a gym or studio, and a year later we quit and cancel the subscription. We begin to walk or run and at some point, then we quit, due to boredom, injury, chronic pains, disease or overwork.

Many people do not carry out any activity, usually due to their perceived physical condition, but sometimes also due to financial or social circumstances. Even those who do carry out some sort of activity, for the most part, limit themselves to minimal activity within their comfort zone such as walking, swimming or yoga, and do so in an agonizingly slow manner, without developing any muscle mass, speed, balance, posture or coordination, or practicing all-out situations. This activity takes place in prolonged time blocks which require reserving slots in the daily and weekly schedule.

How, then, can we maintain a regular level of daily activity that will neutralize the limitations of the training method, and enable us to persevere in physical activity? Selecting the training method also requires the selection of a trainer. Just as with physicians, different trainers have varying levels of knowledge and expertise. There are excellent trainers who can help you, and bad trainers who can harm you. The problem with relying upon a trainer, even an excellent trainer, is that his instructions replace your own thinking and intuition.

There is no training and there are no trainers in nature. Rather, there is a dynamic and constantly-challenging environment, and constant movement, in accordance with circumstances and intuition, regardless of time blocks. This is why the super-exercise training model is highly varied, dynamic and spontaneous activity, based on all motion components, without committing to any particular pattern or method, without trainers, and without any hierarchical ranks. The individual is his own trainer. These principles can be implemented on any type of training or exercise and we will expand upon this later on.

1.6 SIXTH VARIABLE – DOSAGE

Almost every activity in life is characterized by some dosage. For example, my work dosage is 30 hours a week; I drink coffee at a dosage of 3 cups per day; I sleep at a dosage of 7 hours every night. Likewise, in order to prepare a closet, the carpenter requires a precise "dosage" of lumber of a given size.

That is why when we consider physical activity - walking, running, boxing or swimming - the need to refer to the familiar dosage variables immediately arises within us: How frequently should the exercise/training be repeated? For how long? At what intensity? At what speed? How much should we rest? How many repetitions? What is the minimum effective dose?

There are two quite common dosage mistakes. The first is overdosing, a common mistake of professional sports. Many athletes train for long hours every day and suffer as a result from injuries and accelerated bodily deterioration. The second, far more common mistake is that of underdosing which is failure to perform sufficient physical activity or any activity whatsoever.

So what is the truly correct dosage? The fitness world is filled with various outlandish dosage recommendations, which are quite often contradictory. In weightlifting, for example, certain schools of thought support a small number of repeats with a high weight burden, whereas another school of thought supports a large number of repeats with a lower weight burden.

Some schools of thought support four training sessions a week, whereas others support once-a-week training. The average trainee usually has no idea what optimal dosage is, and unfortunately, most trainers also lack clear and accurate knowledge about the correct dosage for their trainees. In many cases, the dosage is primarily determined by such factors as the time constraints of the trainee, or a rather arbitrary decision by the trainer.

IN SUPER-EXERCISE THE DOSAGE IS CLEAR – JUST AS IN NATURE: EVERY DAY, ALL DAY.

Using the super-exercise method, the trainee chooses and determines intuitively and spontaneously each parameter of dosage. The intensity, duration, repetitions, and variations are all decided and performed in real time as the workout unfolds.

That is precisely how animals and children operate. Animals and children do not move through space in accordance to the instructions of the trainer or the manual written by a physical fitness guru. Their actions are spontaneous and intuitive and depend solely on their immediate environment. When we connect to this child-space and enable it to direct the dosage of our movement, we awaken our inner animalistic nature. The spontaneous dosage is part of the principle of super-freedom, which I will expand upon later. This system does not conflict with structured, time-defined, known intensity and reps training, but I do recommend keeping most physical training spontaneous. This is particularly true for the third age and for people who are just starting physical training after a long break. When the body determines the dosage, it will usually be the correct dosage for the individual at that particular moment. At the same time, I recommend flirting with your comfort zone at least once a day – that is, perform a given exercise a sufficient number of repetitions, or over enough time to feel your muscle burn, or until your heartbeat and respiratory rates increase.

People interested in developing athletic abilities can, of course, totally crush their comfort zone with super-exercises of varying intensity.

The comfort zone boundary can be reached within only two seconds during the isometric towel pulling super-exercise (presented in Chapter 3), and within ten seconds of sprinting in place, you will feel your heartbeat reach new heights. For those who jump, crossing the comfort zone is achieved when you feel your leg muscles ache a bit. When you lift kettlebells, the comfort zone is breached when you begin to feel muscle fatigue or pain, whereas in a pull-up bar hang exercise, one simply hangs as long as possible in order to cross the comfort zone.

1.7 SEVENTH VARIABLE - TIME

Time ticks forward inexorably. Within a few years we will grow old and reach the third age. Some of us are already there. The rules change in the third age. The aging process takes its toll, and most people gradually cease to seek movement, until they gradually lose the ability to do so - sometimes completely - even though they are often still defined as "healthy." Most trainees have short-term goals which do not span their entire lifetime. However, every movement method must take into account the eventual third age.

After all, the most important goal for most of us, particularly in the third age, is freedom from illness and pain. That is why we must identify a movement system that will preserve all movement components throughout our life, and not just in our youth. Physical activity must be examined throughout the entire life cycle and our goal must be to constantly strive to improve over time. From this perspective, training that might lead to injury or degradation over time is a bad idea. So is training that is difficult to persevere in over time. Short term goals, such as losing weight, shaping our body, or getting in shape, no longer seem significant when you examine them with the perspective of the entire life cycle in mind.

When we are young, the passing years don't have much meaning. We work, we have fun, we run, we surf, and we enjoy our life. But these wondrous years fly by, and even those of us who live long often arrive at our final years exhausted, and with an extremely limited and painful range of motion. Can we prevent this age funnel, which only grows narrower from decade to decade, as we lose more and more physical capabilities?

Super-exercise training was designed to halt and even reverse this supposedly inevitable decline. The super-exercises are structured for performance at any age, and even enable improvement over the years.

As mentioned previously, the child's movement is animalistic in character, lacking any rules, is spontaneous, intuitive, and never performed in straight lines. In contrast, we adults move and change positions mostly in accordance to rules and the instructions of trainers and, over time, converge into monotonous motions performed within our comfort zone, in a straight line, within rectangular structures.

As you will discover in the next chapter, the training model of the super-exercises is based on the movement characteristics of children and animals, and aspires to return these natural characteristics to our movement.

1.8 EIGHTH VARIABLE – BREATHING

Breathing is an automatic movement that accompanies us throughout our lives. Supposedly this is not related to training, as it occurs on its own in any event. Nonetheless, there are various ways to cultivate our breathing and add an important layer to our training. In the Western world, mouth breathing, sleep apnea, stuffed noses, hyperventilation, and weak diaphragm are common problems. Such weakness results in impaired breathing. When our breath is inefficient, all the organs of our body suffer and age at a faster rate.

Without proper delivery of oxygen-rich blood and without a strong and supple diaphragm, both our physical and mental performance will be sub-optimal. That is why paying special attention to our breath is an extremely important part of this system.

In the super-exercise training model we will work on improving and training and strengthening the chest and diaphragm muscles, so that they will efficiently support every activity we undertake.

CHAPTER 2

The Philosophy of Super-Exercise Training

Ground, water, trees, strength, speed, coordination, balance, flexibility, endurance, posture, brain, breathing, personal health, nutritional, economic and psychological conditions, goals, training methods, dosage, time … So many variables.

What does one do with all these variables? How can they be shaped into physical movement that will not only enable you to develop a strong and wise body, but will also preserve the body's physical fitness and your health throughout your entire life cycle, and perhaps even improve it? As we have seen, physical movement is an extremely complex challenge, and working out in the gym three times a week is not enough to crack it and achieve our goals.

Now that we have broken down the central components of physical movement and examined their characteristics, in the current chapter we will explain the philosophy and the principles behind the super-exercise training model. The model is based on combining these components, and how each component can be implemented within the model.

2.1 IMPLEMENTING THE FIRST VARIABLE – MOVEMENT ENVIRONMENT

The first basic rule in the super-exercise training model refers to the movement environment variable. To fully realize the potential contained within our musculoskeletal system and brain, we must seek, regardless of the training regime we selected, to move **in all three environments** where our body evolved – ground, water and trees.

In each of these environments, the body utilizes a different neuromuscular array that is imprinted in each of us. We all know how our body operates in the ground environment, but when we swim or climb, completely different neuromuscular arrays are activated.

For example, when we dive, the body's diving reflex is triggered. The skin is subject to increased atmospheric pressure and breathing halts, and the body is operating in a nearly weightless, but high friction environment – precisely the opposite of ground movement.

During climbing, the body breaks down the harmony of movement into motion reminiscent of a drummer. When climbing, each of our limbs is always doing something else and moving in a unique way.

Performing water movements poses a significant challenge for most people. There are those who own or live near a pool or a lake and can swim every day. Such a body of water is not always geographically accessible, though, or the usage fee is too high, as may be the case with public pools. Nonetheless, I recommend you try to find a solution that will enable you to swim and train in a water environment as often as possible – without, of course, neglecting the other two environments.

How should one move in the marine environment? When we think about movement in water, the image most of us have is of swimming from wall to wall utilizing the breaststroke, crawl, backstroke, or butterfly styles. This is the classic movement performed by fixated, serious adults; a predetermined monotonous movement which occurs within a rectangle and proceeds only forward in a straight line.

To free us from this fixation, I recommend you watch dolphins or children in water. Their movements are never repetitive, they move in all directions, and their facial expressions reflect their extraordinary joy from their activity – a gameplay expression, as opposed to the grave demeanor of a swimmer advancing to the finish line. Later, we will see how one can move in the water environment in a creative, enjoyable and wise manner. In addition, one can perform "watery" movements on the ground, such as the wave movement of the spinal cord that appears in several qigong exercises (for example, the shoulder movement exercise appearing in Chapter 3.)

The climbing environment is much easier to implement. One can still find tree branches almost everywhere, as well as playgrounds. Even those who lack playgrounds and trees in their environment can easily and inexpensively install a pull-up bar at home, in their yard or in the workplace. The motion characteristic of climbing is, as aforementioned, the grip — the grasping of fingers around the branch or the bar — and pulling or holding the body up by the power of the hand. The integration of the climbing element in the daily routine is an important part of improving your physical fitness.

PRACTICING OUTSIDE, RATHER THAN IN BOXLIKE STRUCTURES

In the previous chapter we discussed how one of the blocks invented by the fitness industry, one that has replaced the natural ground, water, and trees environments, is the structural block – such structures as the gym, the soccer and basketball courts, the pool or the studio. In contrast to these human inventions, evolution, genetics and science all converge on a single unambiguous recommendation:

Perform your physical activity outdoors, in the fresh air and the beneficial sun. Try to bring your skin and eyes in contact with the sun as much as possible, without barriers such as sunscreen or sunglasses. Do so wisely, cautiously, gradually and for measured periods of time, to avoid overexposure.

Fitness activity outdoors immediately augments our workout routine with the constantly-changing environment of nature. Walking near the sea or the ocean brings your foot into contact with ground that is slightly different in its angle and rigidity. This information is constantly transmitted to your brain, via special sensors in your foot, and in response the brain must constantly make small changes to the body, and also carefully pay attention to where you are walking. Climbing up a mountainous trail will also confront the body with another type of soil – inclined and slightly different with every step. Under these conditions, the brain is far more alert and focused, for the dangers of mountainous terrain are myriad – pitfalls, steep slopes, loose stones, even wild animals. Outdoor activities stimulate our mind and, at the same time, enable us to soak up some sunlight and the earth's magnetic field, particularly if we are barefoot or swimming in an ocean or a lake.

Going outdoors enables us to interact with the surrounding objects. Even in a purely urban environment, one can raise one's head and find benches, tree branches, beams, stones that can be picked up and thrown, low walls, playgrounds and more. Every object in your environment can fit into your activity. For example, you can grip the tree in the garden or the park with both hands and use it to support yourself as you perform squats. You can lean on the tree and perform standing push-ups on it, or even try a one-armed standing push-up. You can also assume a boxing position facing the tree and pound it a bit (trees are very forgiving, and never punch back) with your open palm as if you were slapping it. The qigong exercises, which were developed through motion in nature, are an excellent opportunity to plant your bare feet safely on the ground, turn to the sun (think of the sphinx in Egypt who turns to the rising sun while planted in the earth), and perform deep breathing exercises while stretching your body and devouring the sun.

2.2 IMPLEMENTING THE SECOND VARIABLE - CHARACTERISTICS OF ANIMALISTIC MOVEMENT

The super-exercise model seeks to restore as many animalistic movement characteristics into our daily activity as we can. That is how our distant ancestors moved, and it was during these times that the genetic and neural infrastructure of our movements were designed. That is where the concept of "every day, all day, every which way, for your entire life, wherever you are" is derived from.

Daily variation is a basic principle of the super-exercise training model. In order to imitate natural animal movements, it is important to meticulously and constantly vary every exercise, training session and training parameter, and also to spice up your physical activity recipe with just a whiff of danger, in order to raise your alertness and improve your instincts and attentiveness to your body and environment.

I do not recommend, of course, that you book a flight to a war zone, but I do recommend you perform a physical activity barefoot (there is a danger you might step on a piece of glass or a nail), rapidly transfer a kettlebell from hand to hand (a danger you might drop the kettlebell on your foot or on the tiles), or occasionally exercise with your eyes closed. Exercises associated with higher risks such as boxing, skateboarding, surfing, high-speed snowboarding and so forth are generally reserved for younger athletes.

I also recommend performing all-out exercises daily, and the book will later present examples of such exercises. As mentioned above, I recommend moving your body as much as possible under the open sky, rather than within sterile blocks.

2.3 IMPLEMENTING THE THIRD VARIABLE – COMPONENTS OF PHYSICAL MOVEMENT

The third variable of the super-exercise training model is the components of the physical movement. It is particularly important to daily implement all components of physical movement – speed, strength, flexibility, balance, coordination, endurance and posture. In fact, this is quite easy to execute, even though most current training methods do not do so satisfactorily.

Other training methods emphasize certain movement components, but completely neglect other components. Body builders and weightlifters emphasize strength and posture to the exclusion of all else such as movement range, coordination, balance, speed and endurance. Long-distance runners emphasize endurance and strengthening the leg muscles while coordination, balance, flexibility, upper body strength and rapid movement are all neglected. Over the years, without even noticing it, we lose elements of movement. Almost all of us, no exceptions, lose the element of speed, and many people already lose it during their middle-age years. The element of coordination also slowly declines over the years, and with it comes the loss of flexibility and balance. That is why, over the years, most people make do with simple movements which do not address even a single component; for example, monotonous walking in a block. In super-exercises training, the goal is to train with each of these components, and not leave any of them out of the picture. As you will discover, this goal can be achieved relatively easily by wise selection of exercises and movements.

A wise selection of movements assigns your brain with an important and active role. Our aspiration is to keep it constantly engaged with our physical activity. A simple way to engage your brain is through diversification, which the super-exercises method encourages.

When the trainee determines the diversity of the workout on their own, the brain must remain engaged. Constant diversity of movement will result in the formation of new brain synapses and, as my clinical experience teaches, brain function improves remarkably in fields unrelated to physical activity.

2.4 IMPLEMENTING THE FOURTH COMPONENT – THE TRAINEE

As we discovered, the number of variables associated with the trainee is incredible: health condition, nutrition, sleep quality, intelligence, socioeconomic status, beliefs, and goals. All of these, plus many other variables, fulfill important functions in how we move, and in the nature and effectiveness of the movement.

In accordance with the spirit of this method, I recommend bypassing all the variables and myths associated with physical activity and focusing on only one variable – wise selection of goals. Below I present several worthy goals – as well as less worthy goals:

WORTHY GOALS

- I want to be in excellent physical shape, with a muscular, flexible, swiftly-responding body, free of pain and illness
- I wish to preserve all movement components throughout my life, and even improve them over time
- I want to move wisely and efficiently every day, all day
- I want to make wise and successful decisions about my health, such as eating healthy food, sleeping well, getting exposure to sunlight, and avoiding environmental toxins
- I want to understand what impacts my health and what I can do about it

LESS WORTHY GOALS

- I must get in shape – a vague goal underlined by guilt, leading you to enter a difficult training regime which unfortunately usually ends with injuries or burnout, and possibly a visit to the orthopedic surgeon
- I must keep up with social media – this goal is so deeply embedded in all of us, that it leads us to waste much of our day sitting in front of screens and harming both our bodies and our brains
- I must lose weight – this is a goal which only a few percent of the population can achieve or preserve over time and trying and failing only makes us miserable
- I need to go to the doctor to "fix" my pain

The super-exercise model is designed so that regardless of what your personal variables are – how old you are, how much money or free time you have, or how healthy, ill, thin or chubby you are – you can implement and perform the exercises successfully. Even if you lack any motivation whatsoever and have no desire or ability to move your bodies, I recommend a daily performance of super-exercises. Keep tending the embers, and one day they will flare back to life.

2.5 IMPLEMENTING THE FIFTH VARIABLE – THE TRAINING

Super-exercise training includes a vast variety of carefully selected exercises. The criteria I set for their selection were quite strict: they had to be

— easy to learn
— simple to execute
— completely safe to perform

— accessible at any time, any place and at any age
— contain all three movement environments – earth, water and trees, and all animalistic movement characteristics, and all human physical movement components.

An exercise that meets all these criteria is what I call a super-exercise.

In the next chapter, I will present you with these exercises. Before I do, however, it is important to realize that how we approach the exercise is even more important than the exercise itself. Since the training method is completely free, I call the spirit of the method "super-free." The approach underlying the model is liberated, spontaneous, intuitive, and childlike, and the movement is therefore, by definition, highly varied in every parameter.

You will be the ones to determine the time you practice, the type of exercise and its dosage. The method calls upon the trainee to constantly study and change the parameters of his movement.

For example, if you are walking in a straight line at a constant pace for a predetermined distance on a predetermined day, then you can fill the half hour you are in any event spending on walking, with a nearly-infinite wealth of movement by changing almost every possible parameter. You can, for example, walk slowly or rapidly. You can jump as you walk, either on one leg or on both. You can wave your hands wildly at all sorts of angles, close your eyes for a brief moment, or perhaps walk barefoot (additional possibilities will be presented in Chapter 3). Similarly, if you swim in a straight line like most adults, start swimming like a child or a dolphin – leap in the water, dive into the water or dance. Vary your swimming in every possible way. Every motion, and certainly every super-exercise, is a portal to endless variations that are based on constant change and variety. Some of the most intrinsically varied activities, such as skateboarding, acrobatics, snowboarding and dancing, are not accessible to most of the population.

They are simply too complex, and for many of us too dangerous. Nevertheless, this does not mean we need to give up variety in motion and make do with monotonous activities.

Even if you never perform even a single super-exercise from the repertoire presented in the next chapter, you can still implement the principle of variation in your training – regardless of what type of activity you choose and how monotonous and simple it may be – and thereby enrich your movement and render it happier and more spontaneous.

Slowly, the neural networking in your brain and muscles will evolve and develop in such a way that you will be astonished at how swiftly your mind and body shed their limiting fixations, and how rich the repertoire of your physical motion becomes.

2.6 IMPLEMENTING THE SIXTH VARIABLE - DOSAGE

The dosage of super-exercises is simple. Just like the movement of animals and children, the rule is every day, all day, for your entire life. When a certain exercise or movement is performed every day, the nervous system slowly imprints the movement within it, making it more effective.

The duration of the training, the type of exercises, their order, and the intensity of the training are all determined in a spontaneous manner by the trainee. The minimum time per training session is three seconds (in an isometric towel-pulling exercise, for example) and the maximum is several minutes. The idea is to perform super-short exercises of several seconds to several minutes throughout the day, repeatedly. During each of the training sessions we will perform a given super-exercise or a sequence of several super-exercises. The system is not, of course, limited to the exercises presented in the book. You can select any motion or type of training and perform it as well spontaneously for a short period of time.

However, the great advantage of super-exercises is that they are designed and selected to be suitable for performance anytime and anywhere.

Moreover, since the training duration is so short, I recommend you perform the best possible exercise in this short duration. This will maximize the return on investment. If you have 10 seconds, it is better to perform 3 squats than walking. The training session repertoire will be new and different on every day, in accordance to your spontaneous decisions. You may, for example, train for 10 seconds in jumping jacks, and then train for 5 seconds hanging from a bar, and then perform an isometric exercise for 3 seconds. On another occasion, you can practice with the kettlebells for two minutes, and then perform a single pull-up and later do the shoulder delight exercise and then jump for half a minute. Throughout the day, you can accumulate several short training sessions this way.

The short period of the training session along with the simplicity of the exercises will enable you to move your body and perform the exercises for dozens and even hundreds of repetitions throughout your usual workday, with minimal investment of time. For example, if you jump for 10 seconds, you can perform about 20 jumps. If you repeat this 10 times throughout the day, then you will have jumped a total of 200 times that day – you moved your body in an exercise which incorporates many activity components and performed it 200 times, while investing no more than 100 seconds, scattered across tiny 10-second intervals. Since this is a short interval, it is easy and simple to perform spontaneously, regardless of where you are. This trait is shared by most super-exercises – you can perform them wherever you happen to be at any given moment.

I recommend that you vary and constantly change the order of the exercises, their intensity, the length of the training, and the time of day at which you perform them. Change every conceivable detail in the training, so that each day looks different in terms of the time when you trained, the exercises, the length of the training and its intensity. Change and diversity themselves will, paradoxically, become the constant variable. Once you realize that you are not planning the next day's activity and do not recall the previous day's activity, then this is a sign you are training in the spirit of the system.

"A 10- or 20-second training session? How can that help me, Doctor?" I hear this question from my patients repeatedly when I present the concept to them.

It is true that for body builders or long-distance runners, this 10-second training sounds like a joke. Even if these 10 seconds are repeated 20 times a day, this is still a 200 second training – 3 minutes and 20 seconds. "Come on, Doctor, you can't be serious." One of the most prevalent myths regarding physical activity says that the longer we train, the more fit we will get: 'No pain, no gain.' But that myth was created by professional athletes, for whom physical activity and competitions are a career. That is why they must push themselves to excel, but it also leads them to injure themselves and wears down their joints.

For those of us who are not athletes, the myth of prolonged training is just not right. Most people sit for many hours a day. Ninety percent of the time, they provide the body with a very monotonous stimulation of sitting in a chair, and then perform concentrated training two or three times a week. However, research has shown that two or three training blocks a week are not nearly enough to counter the harmful influence of prolonged sitting. That is why the current recommendation is to stand up every few minutes and loosen up your body. That is precisely the opportunity to perform one or more super-exercises, instead of merely standing. By the way, that is precisely how apes perform their activities – in short bursts that are scattered throughout the day.

What are the advantages of training sessions lasting only 10 seconds? First, this short time period requires no preparatory organization or clearing a window of time in our schedules. Second, when we are training for a short period of time, there is no danger of being bored. It is impossible to be bored from any activity that lasts only 10 seconds. That is why such training can also be suitable for children that have short attention spans.

A 10-second training does not require any special motivation, only a glimmer of willpower and awareness and presto: 10 seconds and the super-exercise is done. Ten seconds also mean little effort or stamina are required, for the impact on the body is very small. A super-short training is the way to bridge between complete inactivity and prolonged physical activity over long blocks of time. Even an individual with an extremely busy schedule will not find it difficult to clear 10 seconds off his calendar, and even very ill people afflicted with various pains can certainly do bursts of activity of 4-5 seconds without suffering any harmful side effects.

The short time span constitutes the lowest common denominator: everyone can handle such a short exercise, regardless of the composition of the various other variables in their individual activity. A 10-second training enables those who want to "start working out" or "make a change in their life," to truly and immediately embark on achieving their goals. A 10-second burst is a base from which one can easily progress.

A young, athletic man or woman can of course take these super-exercises and structure them into a longer and more difficult training session, especially if he or she incorporates bodyweight exercises - weights, athletic jumps and more - while working the body in varying intensity intervals (more on that in Chapter 9). If, on the other hand, you are 40 years old or older, I recommend you do not test the limit of your abilities, but content yourself with playing with your comfort zone in order to preserve your joints and bones in good enough shape to last your third age. Where can a 40-year-old man who runs marathons and triathlons and trains 1-2 hours everyday progress to? At this stage he has reached the pinnacle of his training. When he hits 50, he will have to slow down, slow it down further at 60, and by the time he hits 80, most chances are he will do nothing but nurse the injuries he has accumulated over the years.

On the other hand, a 40-year-old individual who begins exercising 10 seconds every day, and adds 10 additional seconds of daily training every month, will be performing 2 minutes of activity a day by the end of the year, will be exercising 20 minutes a day by age 50, and by age 80 he will reach 80 minutes of training each day. The monthly addition of time and effort are negligible, but over the years, the exertion scale gradually becomes more demanding, albeit at a snail's pace.

What this means is that our bodies will undergo a slow but consistent adaptation, and this is one of the ways we can improve throughout our life cycle.

Go back to observing animals and children. Note how movement in nature is flowing, responsive, flexible, and unbound by any law, pattern or set time frame. Animals and children naturally avoid excessive exercise which might injure them, and you will almost never see them contort their faces in agony while moving.

In the next chapter, I will present to you a variety of super-exercises and explain precisely how each must be performed. In the meantime, however, see below an example of a short exercise regimen which includes 12 ten-second exercises:

- A simple stretch on a pull up bar for 10 seconds
- Rebounding for 10 seconds (about 20 jumps)
- Five squats
- Two three-to-four second-long isometric exercises

- An "all-out" sprint in place
- Three athletic jumps
- Bear walk
- Six kettlebell swings
- Four back-and-forth rolls on rings
- Five push-ups
- An all-body stretching exercise, such as a shoulder roll
- Twenty rapid shadow boxing punches in the air

These 12 exercises contain all the physical activity components. They enable a short visit to the limit of your comfort zone. You have performed one all-out exercise and stretched your body well – and all this in only 2 minutes a day that are divided into a dozen 10-second segments each.

The length of the segments is also a variable subject to constant changes – in accordance with decisions made in advance, according to your mood, or when you grow tired. Every time you exercise, the length of the segment will differ than the one that precedes or follows it. This will happen automatically if you stop glancing at the clock. It is enough that you lengthen the training from 10 to 30 seconds in order to gain 6 minutes a day without reserving any time for this, without dressing up in your training clothes, without traveling to a special destination for this – and without paying anyone for the privilege of working out your own body.

The super-exercise training method enables us to train throughout the day, covering all the components of movement spontaneously. It is done in short durations and therefore with minimal stress on the body. Since the exercises are performed wherever you are, and regardless of your situation, you won't even feel you had to make an effort to work out and exercise. This type of training does not require motivation or pre-planning, and it only takes up a few minutes every day.

Since you are performing the exercises on a daily basis, your body will adjust well to every exercise, in a slow and injury-safe manner, and can easily withstand a slight increase in intensity. Walk this path, and you will feel how you improve year by year – you will gain greater familiarity with the simple exercises, begin to train more times per day, and as your body becomes better trained, you will be able to perform more and more variations. You will slowly push back the limits of your comfort zone, enabling you to occasionally to press harder on the intensity pedal.

You will slowly be able to build up your body with a variety of abilities and movements that are not fixated on any particular type of sport. Once you train with all the movement components unexpectedly and changeably, from day to day, your body will learn how to adapt to the change and constantly become more robust, strong and energetic. On a deeper cognitive and emotional layer, you imprint yourself with a vision while making this passage. You start to view physical movement from a holistic perspective. You start visualizing yourself moving throughout your lifecycle. You understand deeply that this is the only way to cultivate holistic movement and preserve and improve your physical capacities.

Take for example Joseph. At 82, he still works and trains every single day. At his last clinic visit, he bragged about some really cool exercises he can do. "Show me," I told him. He smiled, dropped straight down to the floor, laid down on his back and flicked his legs over his head, touching his knees to his ears and pressing his feet to the floor behind his head. He came back to sitting and rolled right back with total nonchalance on the hard tiles. A perfect rollover.

Joseph could pull off this stunt that even a 20-year-old might find difficult because he had practiced it for 50 years straight, on a daily basis, and because he enjoys viewing himself as successful and ageless. The exercise itself takes five seconds to perform and requires no warmup. Joseph's rollover does not qualify as a super-exercise since it is not 100 percent safe and certainly not everyone can do it, let alone older people. Yet this exercise was done according to method. Every day, all his life.

Imagine yourself adopting only one exercise and committing to performing it every day for the rest of your life. Imagine yourself 50, 40, 30, 20, or 10 years from now depending on your current age, still doing this exercise, becoming better and better, slowly but surely and then impressing your 80-year old friends or knocking the socks off your grandchildren with a display of doing 40 push-ups or 150 rope jumps or performing a perfect qigong stretch. This means choosing a short, simple and highly effective super exercise rather than choosing a whole method like yoga, or lengthy exhausting running which makes movement readily available and way easier to preform for just about anybody.

Due to the strict criteria I mentioned, the model contains only a limited number of super-exercises, but you are more than welcome to perform any exercise you feel like, while maintaining the spirit of constant change and the dosage – every day, all day, for the rest of your life.

2.7 IMPLEMENTING THE SEVENTH VARIABLE – TIME

In many modern training methods, movement is only performed accompanied by a trainer who prepares a training program for the trainees. In most cases, and particularly for beginners, the training program will include an exertion scale. Both the trainer and the trainee are usually interested in a rapid exertion scale, for they aspire to achieve rapid results – weight loss, improvement in fitness, or more muscle mass. Most of us want to acquire skills rapidly and improve quickly. In various sports, the push to improve efforts is constant, and the aspiration is to achieve improvement within months. The trainers exhort the trainees constantly, and also present a personal example via their own bodies.

Other training methods suffer from the opposite problem – monotonous training which does not progress. The exertion scale in these methods is zero. For example, if you do yoga twice a week, or a five-kilometer run three times a week where the training is repeated precisely each week, there is no exertion scale or attempt to improve oneself.

Both of these situations – an overly-rapid exertion scale or the complete absence of an exertion scale – are harmful to the trainee. In the first situation, the trainee is pushed to seek achievements beyond his capabilities, leading to injury, whereas in the second situation there is no progress, making it only a matter of time until boredom and monotony lead the trainee to abandon the system.

Moreover, neither training pattern takes into account the entire life cycle. Most people do not ask themselves, "What can I do today to maintain my fitness and improve it throughout my life, until I reach old age?"

My stated goal in preparing the super-exercise training model was therefore to manufacture movement that would not only preserve one's abilities throughout his entire lifetime, but which would also **improve** over the years. The exertion scale should stretch over decades, to ensure there is always progress, however slow. Improve over the years? We have grown used to believing that physical activity cannot improve with age, for we inevitably decline with old age.

And that is indeed true for most physical activity methods. I have never seen a soccer player play better at 60 than he did at 30. I never saw anyone swim better at 80 than at 20. Of all the methods and variations of physical activity, only two realize the ability to improve over the years without bouncing off the glass ceiling of chronological age.

Sensei Oshima qualified me for a black belt in karate in 1985. He was the direct pupil of the inventor of the Shotokan karate style Sensei Gichin Funakoshi (1868-1957). Oshima is now 89, and a YouTube video of his from a few years ago impressively illustrates his incredibly precise abilities.

During my travels in China, I met elderly qigong instructors, 80 and 90 years old, who move very impressively. Peaceful martial arts, such as Shotokan karate, tai-chi, and other soft Chinese martial arts, enable those who practice them long years of improving and finessing their movements. In yoga, as well, there are trainees who continue to practice and improve, deep into their elderly years.

The second method which enables improvement throughout the life cycle is strength training with weights. Since these are static exercises that are extremely simple and accessible, any individual, regardless of his or her age, can begin weight training and improve over the years.

All other training methods will, at some point or another, get stuck in the aging funnel and disappear from our repertoire of movement. The problem is that these two methods are only suitable for a rare few.

Serious training in martial arts is only suitable for those capable of persisting in a given method over decades nearly every day of their lives. There are very few such people. Weight training is monotonous and extremely boring, which is why few people will persist in it either.

That is why I structured the super-exercise model to include many elements from martial arts, yoga and weightlifting. These elements, which I knew would enable trainees to perform them throughout their life and even improve in them over time, are incorporated into the daily training in a light and brief way. In this manner, the model enables us to bypass the challenges of serious martial arts training, or persisting with continuous, monotonous, weightlifting training.

Preserving our range of motion and movement capabilities over the years is a complex challenge, and we must be careful not to burn ourselves out in training that will wear us down and age us before our time. That is why the super-exercise training with its short duration, and the safe nature of the exercises, is based on lessening the burden on the joints. This enables maintaining and improving good movement for many years to come. The several-seconds-long training units form a base from which one can continually improve, at a slow pace. A systemic daily training in small dosages can gradually and slowly blossom into a longer and far more diverse daily training and take the trainee and his body to new and fascinating places.

The emphasis placed on diversity and constant change of the parameters in every training session (time of day, intensity, number of repetitions, the nature of the exercise and more) serves as a basis for improvement throughout the entire life cycle.

In my clinic I frequently meet people who regularly perform physical activity, such as walking or running, but who do not trouble themselves with considering how they might improve their endurance throughout their life, until old age. The case of Ilan (an alias), one of my patients, demonstrates this well. 59-year-old Ilan arrived at my clinic for a consultation regarding the results of his bloodwork. As is common at a visit with a family doctor, we discussed his general health and I questioned him regarding his physical activity.

Ilan runs 5-10 kilometers (3-6 miles) three times a week. He runs in the park or on the beach during regular hours of the evening. He has been running for 10 years now, likes it very much, and says that the running "clears his mind." Recently, he has found it somewhat difficult to run his usual course, due to a slight pain in his knee.

Any doctor would immediately conclude that Ilan was a highly active individual and continue to discuss other matters with him. But was Ilan really active? Was he truly fit? Is he really preserving his health?

Ilan was actually slightly overweight and his upper body seemed rather weak. What was even more problematic was the fact that he had completely lost touch with his body. The body, insofar as he was concerned, was "that thing that runs." Ilan had forgotten, through no fault of his own of course, that his body was designed and constructed to perform far more diverse activity.

I explained to Ilan why our bodies have such great movement potential. I explained to him that animals and children never run in a straight line or in sneakers. I explained that running is a monotonous activity that might wear down the leg joints, that most runners stop running at some point due to injury, loss of strength, boredom or disease, and that it is very rare to find 80-year-old men running three times a week.

I further made clear to him that in spite of his investment in running three times a week, this is not enough to compensate for the long hours he sits without moving his body. I recommended to him that he invest in physical activity that will serve him throughout his entire life, and in which he will also be able to improve over the years, in contrast to running which he will gradually be forced to abandon.

I explained to Ilan what he could do to easily vary his running, instead of running at a set pace, at a regular day, for a set time, and in the same shoes. I described to him the health advantages of the rebounding exercise and explained the all-out exercises and their influence on our mental strength in more detail. In the spirit of the method, I recommended that he begin to train daily, and to do so wherever he might be, by stretching, jumping, and doing isometric exercises, and I provided him with additional reading.

I recommended that Ilan specialize in a number of movements that he would be able to perform easily at age 80 and age 90 as well, so that his age would be indistinguishable to an external observer when he performed them. I used analogies from the animal world, referring to long-living animals such as African grey parrots who live 80-90 years, elephants who live 70 years, and whales who live for up to 200 years.

When we observe such animals move from afar, we cannot distinguish the 70-year-old parrot from the 45-year-old parrot, the 60-year-old elephant from the 20-year-old elephant or the venerable 150-year-old whale from the young 80-year-old whale. Only when one looks closely, can you see wrinkles, scars, etc. that disclose the animal's age.

Exercises such as rebounding; stretches on a pull-up bar, breathing exercises or isometric exercises seem from afar to be completely ageless, in stark contrast to running where the age of the runner is readily apparent even from a distance.

We talked by phone a month later and Ilan told with great excitement that he had seen the light in regard to physical activity. He now jumps a little every day and has also begun trying out the pull-up bar and weights, and that he enjoys it very much. I recommended that he continue to diversify his activity, learn new exercises and take it all slowly, for he has his entire life to improve.

2.8 IMPLEMENTING THE EIGHTH VARIABLE – BREATHING

Breathing exercises do not include almost any movement component, but they constitute a very convenient and accessible portal to greatly improve health.

Breathing exercises can be performed anywhere, including while driving a car or riding in an elevator. Since these are internal exercises, they can also be performed in public, without anyone noticing. In the following chapter, I will present breathing exercises and describe various breathing techniques. Proper breathing is often a neglected area in the fitness world and even in the medical, clinical world.

Make no mistake, proper breathing is an essential, if not the essential, cog in maintaining our fitness and overall health.

Before we turn to the repertoire of super-exercises and learn about them at length, let us pause to review a short summary of the principles of the super-exercise training model as described in this chapter. As I explained, the model is intended to cultivate physical abilities, safeguard them, and improve them slowly throughout our life.

This highly varied exercise repertoire was carefully selected according to the following criteria:

- Easy to learn
- Completely safe to perform
- Can be performed at any age and in any location and at any time
- Exercises that train all components of physical movement.
- The exercise looks ageless

I call an exercise which meets all these criteria a super-exercise.

The basic principles of the model:
- Movement in all three environments to which our body evolved to move in; earth, water and trees/climbing
- Daily variation in the types of exercises, in their duration and intensity level
- Training all movement components
- Moving and training like animals, children and successful agers- every day, all day, every which way, for your entire life.

The exercises are performed every day, all day, for your entire life, in small bursts of several seconds to several minutes, scattered randomly throughout the day.

It is recommended you push the envelope of your comfort zone once per day. In addition, it is recommended you perform an all-out exercise once a day. Finally, perform an activity at least once a day, and more if possible, which requires the involvement of your entire brain. A central characteristic of the super-exercises training model is that the trainee himself spontaneously and intuitively decides upon the training time, its intensity, the selection of exercises, the variation of each exercise, the sequence and the number of repetitions of each exercise. Special attention is given to the variation of the other parameters associated to the training, such as the time of day, the location, indoor or outdoor, the type of weight, before or after a meal, and so forth.

The super-exercise training is an open code. That means that anyone can invent their own super-exercise or borrow from any existing system. I recommend you all engage as much as you like in any physical activity you like. The super-exercise training model is built to be incorporated into any training program or other activity. The ease and diversity of the super-exercises will fill the gaps in your other physical activities regardless of what they are.

Super-exercise training is suitable for anyone, for the nature of the exercises enables even beginners to perform them immediately and successfully without risking injury, and without incorrect and potentially damaging postures.

The super-exercise training model shatters all patterns, myths and prejudices we might have concerning physical activity, and especially the myth that training must take place over long calorie-burning, sweaty, soul-crushing time blocks held inside block-like structures. Instead, the model insists that physical activity should be performed wherever you are at a given moment, and at the precise time you decide to perform it.

Last but not least, the super-exercise training model treats the entire world as one vast playground in which there are infinite opportunities for play. It is inspired by the movement of animals and children that is spontaneous, intuitive and instinctive, and takes place within an ever-changing dynamic environment. It seeks to expose the joy of movement and awaken our intuition regarding movement.

We all wish to reach our third age equipped with a flexible, powerful and pain-free body. The super-exercise training makes good, wise movement accessible to each and every one of us, at any age, any place and any situation, once we learn about it. A daily repetition of a good motion is the best way to preserve it throughout our life cycle.

Our goal is long term and our training is for life. It enables us not only to preserve good motion, but also to improve over the years, regardless of when we begin training.

CHAPTER 3

Super-Exercises

Having outlined the super-exercise model and described the philosophy behind it, I will now, in this chapter, showcase a broad selection of super-exercises. Fourteen types of exercises are presented:

- Jumping in place (rebounding)
- Dead hang and bodyweight exercises on a pull up bar
- Kettlebell and medicine ball exercises
- Isometric exercises
- All-out exercises
- Qigong exercises
- Classic exercises
- Free spontaneous movement exercises
- Breathing exercises
- Animal exercises
- Facial exercises
- Walking, running, swimming
- Tricks and toys
- Fascia/connective tissue exercises

Each of these groups includes a wide variety of exercises. Most can be performed alone, without the help of an instructor or fitness trainer.

Rebounding, simple hanging from a bar, qigong exercises and fascia exercises are particularly good super-exercises and I very much recommend starting out with them, performing them every day and even several times a day.

Rebounding is the best ground exercise, for it gives us a safe taste of the rapid movement of the hunter. Hanging on a bar gives us a taste of the climbing world, and the wave exercises (shoulder movements in the qigong exercises, for example) give us a taste of the movement of the body in water. Fascia exercises preserve healthy and flexible connective tissue throughout our lives. Furthermore, these exercises can also be performed in the final decades of our life, particularly if we know them well via prior daily practice. Daily practice of these super-exercises will preserve good posture throughout our life cycle and would constitute an excellent base for any additional training.

3.1 FIRST CATEGORY - REBOUNDING

Take a water glass and fill it about two-thirds. Walk around a bit with the glass in your hand and observe it. Notice what happens to the water. Then jump with the glass still in your hand – what happens to the water now? Like the glass you filled, water constitutes around two-thirds of your body, and just as the water in the glass is jostled in the glass when you jump, so is the water in your body moved about vigorously when you jump.

As a result, our bodies' lymphatic drainage greatly improves, contributing to rapid cleansing of cellular excretions that are transferred to the lymphatic liquid, improving blood circulation. In addition, the effect of gravity on the body is optimal in the jumping movement and is incorporated with acceleration and slowing movements – a combination that is exclusive to this movement.

In the rebounding exercises our connective tissue operates much like a spring, helping to preserve its elasticity. In fact, rebounding is simply the best super-exercise. If I had to choose only one exercise to take with me to a desert island, this would be the exercise. Additional advantages of this exercise include:

- Always easily available to perform, anywhere in the world including a hotel room or on a plane
- Simple to learn
- Safe from injuries
- Anyone who can stand, at any age, with any health issues, can jump
- Improves balance
- Strengthens bones and prevents osteoporosis
- Harmonious movement by the whole body in the same direction and at the same pace (a unique advantage of this exercise)
- Soothing and relaxing
- Improves concentration and attentiveness disorders
- Reduces anxiety and depression
- Returns the body to an enjoyable and childlike movement
- Exercises every cell of the body as well as all 683 muscles
- Contributes to weight reduction and improvement of body composition - waistline, fat mass and lean muscle mass*
- Reduces blood pressure and improves blood fat levels
- Improves posture
- Trains our speed
- Constitutes a basis for countless other exercises
- Can be performed with the entire family
- Supports physiotherapeutic rehabilitation
- Supports recovery from cancer

- In fact, the rate of calories burned by jumping is much higher than walking and running. Jumping for five minutes on a trampoline is, in terms of calorie-burning, equivalent to almost an hour of walking, but with a much lighter load on all joints, given the trampoline's shock absorption.

These advantages have been proven in a variety of studies performed since the 1980s. Cugusi et al. (2016) identified considerable improvement in body composition, significant decrease in blood pressure levels, improvement in sugar and fat blood profile, improvement in physical activity capability and mood, and reduction of pain in overweight women after 12 weeks of jumping exercises. Similar findings were made in earlier research done by NASA (Bhattacharya, McCutcheon, Schvartz and Greenleaf, 1980) where it was found that rebounding on a trampoline does not overload the joints and the body, and is more metabolically effective for the body than running on a treadmill.

Beyond these important advantages, rebounding immediately transports us to the child=like, dynamic world. The upward jumping motion straightens the body and the dynamic, light movement is immediately translated into internal hormonal changes and neural activity, making us a little happier and younger. This contrasts with the downwards-bending motions typical of sadness and despair, as well as old age.

How to perform jumping exercises:

- During the jump, contract your stomach muscles. This automatically engages your back muscles. The stomach and back muscles will thereby be strengthened, setting the lower back vertebrae in place, and protecting them from wear and tear.

Rebounds - the best two-minute home exercise.

- After a few months or weeks, all according to your personal abilities and fitness, you can vary this routine and incorporate deep squats into the exercise, transforming it into a high intensity athletic jump.
- Alternately, you can perform the jump while rotating in the air 90, 180 or 360 degrees.
- Jumping Jacks: This exercise is named after its inventor, Jack LaLanne, America's first fitness guru of the 20th century, who was also one of the inventors of gyms and gym equipment.
  To perform jumping jacks, stand straight with your feet together, and your arms at the sides of your body. Spring upwards while spreading your legs, and lift your arms upwards from the side of your body. Return to your starting position with a jump and repeat.
- Athletic jumps: Fit people can perform several athletic jumps every day – an excellent exercise that cultivates the elasticity and flexibility of the body, and an excellent way to rapidly reach a high intensity state.

Athletic jumps

Several recommendations for the performance of the exercise:

- It is recommended to start gently, though healthy people should not place any time limits on jumping. The training is completely spontaneous, with the duration of the exercise changing naturally from session to session.
- For those who are unfit or in poor health, it is recommended not to jump for over 30 seconds at a stretch. However, you can perform several jumping sessions per day. After a month or so, you should be able to leap higher and for longer. If you wish to jump for more than a minute, you should do so on a trampoline.
- Be prudent about jumping every day. The constant stimulation will enable your body to fully adapt to this movement thus ensuring its continuation throughout your life.
- I recommend taking your time and slowly building up your body in accordance with its athletic capabilities. Many people are so excited with the exercise that they purchase a trampoline and vigorously jump on it for many minutes every day. After several months, however, it becomes a worthless monument which gathers dust. That is why I recommend jumping a little bit every day in short intervals, in order to avoid burning out, and gradually turn it into a daily habit like brushing your teeth. In fact, the jumping "brushes" the body from within, for the sudden acceleration and deceleration cleans up our blood and lymph vessels from whatever is clinging to their interior walls. One sign of reaching the third age is a general slowing down of blood circulation, which rebounding can counter.
- The number of jumping intervals you perform every day is more important than the duration of any single session. The more jumping stimuli we provide our body during the day, the more quickly it will strengthen.

- Jumping in place is a good way to quickly raise your pulse, especially if intermixed with deep squats or twists while jumping in the air. Pulse-increasing exercises, however, are only intended for people in good shape. The recommendation for older individuals, those with unbalanced blood pressure, and those who are unfit or have a physical handicap of some sort is to perform medical jumps only for the first few months. These are light jumps in which one lifts only the heels a centimeter or two (about ½ inch), and then returns his heels flat to the ground. Try to perform two medical jumps every second.

Medical jumps

- People in good physical condition can immediately vary their jumps.
- A trampoline is the diligent and persistent jumper's best friend. The type of trampoline is not very important – what is most important is safety. Older people can use a supportive railing included with some trampolines. One can also support oneself on a wall near the trampoline. Nonetheless, it is important to jump everywhere, and not merely on the trampoline. Many other sorts of exercises can be performed on the trampoline. In fact, any exercise performed on the trampoline will immediately be imbued with balance maintenance and will activate balance-stabilizing muscles. The trampoline challenges balance and ameliorates mechanical stress on the joints. It thereby enables one to run quickly in place – an excellent exercise to rapidly increase the pulse for a short time, as part as interval exercises.

Remember, jumping is a tool which accompanies you every day of your life. That is why, over time, you will discover that you can spontaneously vary it. I began varying my jumping after about three years in which I jumped in the simplest possible way. The possibilities for variety are infinite. One can also utilize YouTube videos illustrating jumping exercises.

- Jump rope exercises are a great way to achieve intensive calorie burn and accelerate weight loss, but they are not for everybody. For children, this is a wonderful, short, high-intensity training, which has many benefits. The jump rope exercise will build up the tonus of the body at its own rate, and the body itself will soon begin to vary the various jumping parameters.

Jump rope

FINAL WORDS ON REBOUNDING

Jumping is a unique exercise because the movement is 100% perpendicular to the ground. This means that we get the full gravity pull when we jump. It also means that the direction of the movement is up. That is why rebounding is a great antiaging exercise: the direction of aging is down, we stoop and become shorter. We will encounter two more perpendicular super-exercises later on. Together, the three of them form what I call "the non-negotiables."

3.2 SECOND CATEGORY - DEAD HANG AND BODY WEIGHT EXERCISES ON A PULL-UP BAR

The dead hang is an excellent super-exercise for anyone, including super-fit athletes.

Advantages of the exercise:

- Strengthens the grip muscles of our hands. Strengthening our grip muscles gives us a firm handshake, as well as a better lifting, opening and closing capabilities. Measuring the power of the grip with a dynamometer is a precise indicator of future illness and mortality, as was revealed in epidemiological research.
- Hanging daily stimulates the body to be longer and more erect, and accordingly slimmer, too. That is why this is a classic anti-aging exercise. Over the years we tend to grow more bent and wider, particularly if we sit for many hours every day. To fully realize this anti-aging benefit, the exercise must be performed daily, the more times each day the better.
- The dead hang is the best stretch for the body. It gently elongates our connective tissue, relieving tensed knots and cultivating our structural integrity. That is why we will encounter this exercise again in the important fascia connective tissues super-exercises group.
- This exercise serves as preparation for more advanced exercises that work with body weight, such as pull-ups, muscle ups, climbing, and more.
- The exercise immediately places the body in its perfect posture and immediately relieves stress (decompression) from the lower back. That is why it is excellent for those suffering from lower back pain.

- This exercise immediately awakens the "apelike" component of our movement. We need a strong grip and powerful core muscles to climb and move on trees. The daily performance of this exercise will bring about exactly that and will support any other movement or drill you exercise.
- This is a simple exercise that is suitable for any level, any age and any physical condition.

Examples of hanging exercises:

- Hang with straight arms on the bar or on a branch, with your hands at shoulder width or a bit wider, with your palms facing forward and the thumb opposed to the fingers (locked grip). Slowly shift the body weight from the legs to your hands. Stay hanging for several breaths. The exercise lasts several seconds, and I recommend performing it several times a day. You can challenge yourself occasionally and stay hanging for a longer period, quietly counting to 10 or 20, perhaps even to 30. After a few weeks or months, when your grip is stronger, you may choose to swing forward and backwards. Another possibility is to raise your legs as you are hanging.

- You can also begin to flex-hang; that is hanging from the bar with your elbows bent. This exercise will prepare you for pull-ups.
- Later on, after a few months or years – everyone at his own pace, of course – you could aim at managing to pull yourself up a bit and perform a full pull-up. From a hanging state, pull yourselves up, at a steady pace, until your chin reaches the bar.
- I recommend that at first you perform a single pull-up, and change only the speed at which you pull yourself up and descend. A single pull-up is an excellent exercise sufficient onto itself. Later on, you

can increase the number of pull-ups and slowly enter the world of pull-up-bars and rings. The great advantage of this "world" is the complete absence of stress on the lower back and legs. This is an excellent exercise for anyone suffering from orthopedic or neurological problems of the lower body.

- Another exercise which can be used as preparation for pull-ups, as well as an exercise in its own right, is horizontal pull-ups. Grip a bar (or the TRX bands) at chest height or lower. Move a bit forward, until your chest is below the bar, and then straighten and bend your arms, with your feet on the ground.

Various bar exercises can occupy the athletes among us for their entire lives, and I recommend to anyone who wishes to properly develop their body in their teens, and in their 20s and 30s, to persist and deepen their training in this classic climbing movement. The options for progress and improvement are infinite. I myself began to perform pull-up-bar exercises in high school and have been practicing on the high bar for more than 40 years now. Over the years I have grown stronger, and today I perform a series of more difficult exercises such as front levers, jumping from one bar to another, muscle-ups and slowly aiming towards one arm pull-up. My improvement is extremely slow, and there is no need to hurry anywhere. We have our entire lives to improve.

Hanging on a bar is a simple super-exercise and is important to anyone at any age.

The urban environment is packed, perhaps more than you realize, with places where we can hang. Any branch jutting out from a tree is a potential "hanging bar." Unlike the dedicated hanging bar, the angle of tree branches is not, in most cases, parallel to the ground, and the diameter varies across the length of the branch. This is excellent, for this varies the climbing or gripping angle. Exercise equipment in public gardens, iron beams sticking out of walls and various supportive pillars can also serve as hanging bars.

The urban environment is like a giant, free gym, filled with infinite variety that we can plug into whenever we are outdoors. Just like our ancestors, we are in constant contact with the environment, regardless of its shape and location.

One final note. Just like in rebounding, when we dead-hang, our body is perpendicular to the earth throughout the exercise. Repeatedly returning to an erect, tall and harmonious posture counteracts the aging body dynamics which gravitate downward. Hanging frequently will guard your skeleton and connective tissue from the elderly phenotype of a stooped, hunched, low posture. That is why the dead hang is the second non-negotiable super-exercise

3.3 THIRD CATEGORY - KETTLEBELL AND MEDICINE BALLS

Kettlebells and medicine balls are an excellent tool for cultivating dynamic strength. Kettlebells originated in Russia over 300 years ago. These weights, called "girya" in Russian, were in fact an ancient Russian measuring unit used to weigh grain, but became popular amongst harbor men and farmers as a fitness tool. They were adopted by athletes in Russia and Europe in the late 19th century and, as sports legend has it, helped Russian athletes dominate the Olympics in the 1950s.

Jon Bruney, one of the strongest men in the world, invented an entire training method based on kettlebell weights. (For those who wish to expand their repertoire of exercises, I recommend reading Jon Bruney's book "Neuro-Mass: The Ultimate System for Spectacular Strength.") The great advantage of kettlebells, as of the medicine ball, is that they enable dynamic work which involves the entire body. Another important characteristic is that the movement does not take place in a straight line - it is circular. In many exercises, the kettlebell/medicine ball is rapidly and dynamically transferred from hand to hand. Breaking the monotonous line of the movement of classic weight exercises and moving the entire body without isolating muscles, builds a strong body. More importantly, it builds a body which knows how to work in operational coordination.

Weights exercises are not classical super-exercises, for they obviously demand weights. Hence, they cannot be performed everywhere and at any time unless you hang a kettlebell on your belt and take it everywhere you go. Nonetheless, these exercises are suitable for any age and, like jumping and hanging, they are simple to learn, extremely easy to perform, and are very safe. Medicine balls also offer endless potential for excellent exercises. In the spirit of the super-exercise training model, I recommend you leave the blocks and patterns we have all grown used to, and simply train spontaneously with the medicine ball or kettlebells for several seconds. People with athletic goals can reach extraordinary achievements with these tools.

The work I will describe here, just like jumping and hanging, will accompany you every day of your lives. So it is important here as well not to burn out after a few months of excess enthusiasm, and then leave your kettlebell and medicine ball to gather dust in the closet. I keep a 16-kilo (~35 lb) kettlebell and an 8-kilo (~17.5 lb) medicine ball in my clinic, and demonstrate exercises to my patients with them, or train in the short intervals between patients or during my breaks.

Examples of kettlebell/medicine ball exercises include:

- Transfer the kettlebell behind your back from hand to hand, twist it around your body, and then transfer it from hand to hand in front of your body. Perform the exercise several times in one direction and then change direction and perform several more repetitions. The duration of the exercise is 10-30 seconds (see exercises below).

The great advantage of this exercise is that it is extremely easy to perform, and yet it simultaneously enables training of strength, speed, coordination and balance. The exercise immediately places the weight work on a dynamic and coordination-based plane, for the trainee is forced to focus (especially if training at home where dropping the kettlebell might shatter expensive flooring).

3

2

1

6

5

4

The exercise can immediately be varied by performing it with closed eyes or standing on one foot. Alternately, you can try performing the movement as rapidly as possible. This exercise can also be performed with a medicine ball.

- Another exercise I highly recommend is a dynamic exercise in which the weights are bounced from hand to hand while crouching to a squat and rising back up.

Grip the weight in one hand as you crouch in a squat position, and as you rise from the squat, rapidly lift the weight towards your chin. When your hand reaches maximal height, release the weight so that it remains in the air for a split second, and then grab it in your other hand and lower your hand, simultaneously dropping back down to the squat. Repeat. A few months later, once the body is familiarized with the weight, you can vary the exercises almost infinitely. Here, too, you can rely on an impressive collection of YouTube clips

- Another recommended exercise is the swing – swinging the kettlebell back and forth. This exercise is not for beginners or for very old people, but correct, gradual and purposeful training can enable anyone to perform it, and it is considered one of the best body strengthening exercises. Pavel Tsatsouline, a legendary fitness trainer who brought kettlebells to the West from Russia, wrote an entire, popular book on nothing but two kettlebell exercises. One of them is the swing exercise and its plentiful variations, and the other is the "Get Up" exercise.

 Kettlebell clip

- Swing exercise: Stand with legs widely spread, knees bent, and hold the kettlebell between your legs with both hands. Swing the weight forward until the hands are parallel to the floor, about chin height, and lower it back down in a sort of a swing motion, until it returns between your legs and even reaches behind your pelvis, and repeat. Keep your chest upright and your stomach clenched in.

Swing exercise

Several recommendations on performing the exercises:

- Perform the kettlebell/medicine ball exercises in the spirit of the method. That means brief intervals of 10-30 seconds.
- "Mine" your home and office with several kettlebell and medicine ball weights. If there is no readily available kettlebell weight, the exercises can also be performed with a regular hand weight.
- The kettlebell weight generally recommended to an adult beginner is 6-8 kilograms (13-17.5 lb), but the weight changes, of course, from individual to individual. In the first few months I recommend you practice with a weight relatively easy for you, even if you think you can tackle a heavier weight. Remember, this is an exercise for life, so there is no reason to hurry. A lighter weight will cause the body to adopt and construct a stable foundation, from which you can begin to diversify and raise the kettlebell's weight gradually. I began with a light, 8-kilo weight and worked with it for a year before I progressed to a heavier weight. I now work in the spirit of the system with a variety of weights, of which the heaviest is 20 kilograms (44 lb), but I occasionally enjoy returning to my 8 kilogram weight and training with it in a spontaneous motion, without making much effort.
- In the third age, I recommend practicing simple, easy-to-perform exercises. If you still wish to progress to heavier weights or to more difficult exercises, do so with the aid of a trainer.
- In order to diversify training with the kettlebell and medicine ball, make use of the numerous videos on YouTube.

Final note: Weights are quantifiable and, as such, can be easily tracked. Tracking helps make this form of training life-long, since we can see our progress year-by-year and decade-by-decade as we slowly but surely advance to slightly heavier weights.

3.4 FOURTH CATEGORY - ISOMETRIC EXERCISES

Alexander Zass (1888-1962) was a Russian soldier during World War I. He had been involved in bodybuilding before the war. He was captured by the Austro-Hungarians four times during the war, and each time was able to escape. The POW camp was not the ideal site for body-building training, so Zass resorted to "training" by pulling bars and chains with all his power and strength. To his astonishment, he discovered that his body had grown so strong that he could escape the prison camp by bending the bars and breaking the chains holding him in. After the war, he launched a career of strength demonstrations in circuses and was called "The Amazing Samson," "The Iron Samson" or just "Samson." As part of his circus performance, he carried two lions on his back, caught women fired out of a cannon, hung a piano from his teeth, and performed various other feats of strength inspired by his training in prison camps. His recommendation to everyone was to engage in isometric training.

Isometric training is based on contracting muscles with all your force without engaging in any movement whatsoever. The most familiar example of such an exercise is the arm-wrestling contest, in which we can see two evenly-matched people exerting themselves, the veins in their foreheads popping, without any visible movement of their hands. The isometric exercise works solely on the strength of the muscle, and not any other component. That is why it is not considered to be a classical super-exercise. However, in the availability criteria, it is first place amongst all of the exercises and movements, for it truly is available for everyone, in any place and in any age. Isometric exercises are in fact the safest exercises, for no movement is performed and one cannot go wrong. Every time you clench your muscle without moving, that is in fact an isometric exercise. This is the shortest exercise I know. Within a few seconds, the brain recruits the entire depth of the muscle for action, but not for movement. This is an exercise that enlists all the types of muscle fibers - slow and fast - which is why it supports all athletic skills.

Isometric exercises are also the fastest and shortest way to an all-out situation, where we give with all we have — that is, invest our maximal effort. Isometric exercises show up in high-level martial arts. Bruce Lee, for example, had a training routine that included 8 isometric exercises he would perform daily, each exercise for 6-12 seconds. Gymnasts also constantly perform isometric exercises, such as hanging in the cross position on Olympic rings. And yet, in spite of their myriad benefits, most of us have never heard of these exercised, and almost no one performs them.

In the course of modern history, this type of exercises silently disappeared. I hope that they will soon make a reappearance, for these exercises are particularly efficacious in rehabilitating the injured; they enable immediate safe training without moving any limb, which is a particular advantage in the third age. Furthermore, isometric exercises are excellent for those among us who are not fond of sports since one does not even have to rise from the couch in order to perform them.

I recommend to always contract the abdominal muscles (which also leads the lower back muscles to contract) together with other muscles.

Here are a few of my favorite exercises:

- Hang from the high bar with fully extended arms, with hands about shoulder width. The palms can either face the body or face forward, and the thumb is in opposition to the fingers (locked grip). From a hanging position, pull yourselves steadily upwards, but instead of reaching bar height with your chin, stop at some point and remain motionless for a few seconds, until you have had enough. (I usually stay in that position for six-to-eight seconds.)
- Alternately, when you pull yourselves from a hanging position upwards, stop halfway up with elbows bent at 90 degrees and extend your legs forward in a straight angle. Try to remain in that position for several seconds.
- Place hands on the bar, or on TRX bands, with your hands at roughly shoulder width or a bit wider and pull yourselves upwards with the chin reaching, the bar, and stop in this position for several seconds.
- Any exercise can be transformed into an isometric one. All you need to do is halt your body at some point in the exercise and contract as many muscles you can with all your strength.
- Stretch your hands to your sides in the "crucified" position, and then bring them backwards, trying to crush an imaginary ping pong ball between your shoulder blades (see exercise below). This is simply a great exercise that tones your upper back muscles, straightens your spine and opens up your chest.
- Place one wrist on top of the other and push them against each other with all your strength.
- Interlace your hands and try, with all your strength, to push them away from each other.

- You can perform this exercise while sitting in your car, when it is parked of course: Try crushing the steering wheel with both hands, as strongly as you can or, alternately, try to tear the wheel out of place.
- Grab a kettlebell in both hands, with your entire palm gripping the weight, and try to crush it as powerfully as possible.
- Plank in its various permutations is a well-known isometric exercise.

The basic plank exercise (front plank): Lie on your stomach on a mattress. Lift yourselves from the mattress, supporting yourself by your palms and sticking your toes into the floor. Hold yourselves steady for several seconds in this position, so that your body weight is on your arms, elbows, and the tips of your toes. Maintain a straight line between your thighs to the head. This is the basic posture of the exercise, but it can also be performed in other postures, such as side plank and upside down plank, or performed with one leg lifted, and so forth. I like to perform the plank exercise and then jump backwards, forward and to the sides. I do so without deviating from the original position in any way, but merely by making tiny movements in my feet and hands. In this way, an isometric exercise can be incorporated with a small movement.

Another excellent technique, which I have demonstrated to many people with great success, is to perform the plank exercise for only a few seconds, but while maximally contracting every muscle that can be clenched (e.g., abdomen, buttocks) and try to forcefully bring your hands together without moving them. Repeating this simple exercise several times a day will bring about the rapid strengthening of all body muscles. Abdominal muscles are by nature isometric; no movement occurs in the body when we contract only them. As we contract our abdominal muscles, the lower back muscles automatically contract. Under this condition, the central part of the body becomes a rigid cylinder. This cylinder enables optimal power transference from the legs to the hands and vice versa. This cylinder also protects the back vertebrae from small, sudden movements, which might have us visiting the orthopedic surgeon. Increasing the internal abdominal pressure by clenching the stomach muscles can also improve bowel movements.

Daily isometric training of your abdominal muscles is very easy. Simply clench the stomach muscles with all your strength, regardless of your posture, health condition or age. Furthermore, isometric clenching of the stomach muscles should accompany every exercise you perform, regardless of what it is. When you jump, for example, keep your stomach and back muscles clenched tight. When you are training with a kettlebell, keep the central cylinder of the body clenched tight.

TOWEL EXERCISE

Take a long towel, fold it lengthwise and place it on the floor. Stand with your feet on the towel, with legs slightly spread, and grip each side of the towel with your palms. Now, try to pull the edges of the towel upwards, as if you were trying to lift your body. Try to contract every muscle you can muster in the body at once. Three or four seconds of maximized effort will make your muscles burn and bulge. Notice how much your pulse accelerates after such a drill. Many other isometric exercises can of course be developed on your own with a towel.

 Towel pulling isometric exercise

SITTING EXERCISES

- While seated, grip both sides of the chair with your hands and try to lift it with all your strength, much as you did in the towel exercise.

- When you are seated at a table, place your palms beneath the table and try to lift it with all of your strength.

A few recommendations for the performance of the exercises:

- Isometric exercises usually last a single breath.
- When you breathe in, place your body in the position of the exercise. When you exhale, firmly contract the muscles, while hissing out with clenched teeth. By making a hissing sound we increase the pressure on the stomach muscles.
- People with uncontrolled high blood pressure must avoid such exercises, for blood pressure rises in all-out isometric exercises. People with cerebrovascular diseases should also avoid isometric exercises.
- These isometric exercises are ideal for brittle-boned people in their third age suffering from osteoporosis, particularly if they sit all day, for they can be performed in spite of their condition and activate the muscles better than any other exercise.
- The intensity of the exercise should be minimal at first and can be slowly increased, over the course of weeks and months
- Isometric elements can be incorporated in any stretching and flexibility exercise by stopping the movement at any given point, and then clenching the muscle well for several seconds and releasing it. That way we can slightly expand the movement range of the stretch.

There are countless isometric exercises – and you can easily explore this long-neglected training method via Google and YouTube.

As a final note, isometric exercises are unique in the sense that you can perform them inconspicuously, practically anywhere and in any body position, including sitting on your favorite armchair, lying in bed, driving a car etc. While standing in an elevator, for example, you can do a whole-body isometric exercise with opposing wrists, abdominal muscles contraction and pressing your feet together without moving them at all. Boring meetings, long lectures, and waiting in line are opportunities for the best strengthening exercises. Isometric exercises are also the perfect way to enter all-out territory, where the brain pushes the body's pedal to the metal, ordering the muscles to exert themselves to the utmost.

3.5 FIFTH CATEGORY - ALL-OUT EXERCISES

All-out exercises are in fact more of a mental state than an actual exercise. This is an inner state in which we decide, in advance, to put all we have into the exercise. The all-out situation simulates survival. Imagine that you are forced to flee or fight for your life, or you have to lift a heavy object that has fallen on someone, threatening their life. You will surely give everything you have to survive or save your loved one in such a situation.

All-out situations are most common in sport competitions in which the athlete puts everything he has into a brief effort. Most of us experienced this in our childhood, in small-scale sports competitions in school. Some of us may even have experienced this as athletes, but as we grow older, we cease to perform this type of activity, leaving it solely to professional sports and competitions. Unlike us, in nature animals daily experience all-out situations.

All-out situations constitute a critical component in the development of a strong and healthy body. We exert ourselves to the utmost for a brief interval of several seconds, and then breathe more rapidly as our pulse rises. Since this is a survival type of behavior, it trains our nervous system to rapidly recruit maximal muscle mass. It keeps our nervous system flexible, so we will be capable of making rapid changes and adaptations. After an all-out exercise, the nervous system will reach a deeper relaxation in comparison to its previous state, because the body is joyful that we have "survived." An all-out exercise trains and conditions our brain to successfully reach maximum exertion. Over the years, the daily training of all-out conditions will develop internal resources such as determination, perseverance under pressure, willpower, ability to perform and more.

EXAMPLES OF ALL-OUT EXERCISES:

- Perform a rapid sprint in place. Healthy boys and girls, adolescents, men and women can immediately sprint out as fast as they possibly can for a few seconds. Non-athletic or health-challenged people should start with rapid running in place, and gradually increase their pace every month. Be sure to swing your arms forward and backwards rapidly as well, just as in running.
- Perform athletic jumps in the air. Children, youth and healthy adults can immediately try to jump as high as they can, land in a semi-squat and rebound again and again as high as they can, for several jumps.

Simple all-out exercises: running in place and athletic leaps

ISOMETRIC ALL-OUT EXERCISES

Any isometric exercise can be performed in an all-out form. For example, in the towel exercise, envision that you wish to rip the towel as if it were a chain you must shatter to break free. Enlist every muscle in your body, even those you don't really require achieving this purpose. Three to four seconds will suffice to wear you out – a clear sign that you have enlisted all of your muscle mass. In my opinion, this is the fastest way to strengthen all the fibers of your muscles.

Anyone can add this mental component to his routines. I experience this component, for example, when I surf. Rowing on the surfboard to enter the wave is a classic all-out activity. Slowly and moderately pushing the envelope of our comfort zone is one level below an all-out effort. I recommend pushing this comfort zone at least once a day. Any exercise can be taken to the edge of the comfort zone. Some examples would be hanging on a bar until you are out of strength and your muscles ache; bear walking until you are exhausted; jumping until your muscles hurt; swinging the kettlebell until your muscles are sore.

3.6 SIXTH CATEGORY - QIGONG EXERCISES AND POSTURE

I encountered qigong in Israel about 30 years ago, when Master Fong arrived for his first of many visits. I was captivated by the magic of this art, especially given its compatibility with my interest in Chinese medicine and philosophy. The roots of qigong/chi-kung stretch over thousands of years and are inextricably linked to Chinese medicine, developed by ancient sages who discovered hundreds of acupuncture points and thousands of medicinal herbs.

Qigong is based on the traditional Chinese belief that energy, called Chi, flows through our body. Chi means "life energy," whereas kung means "work" or "mission." Literally translated, qigong means controlling the life energies in our body. This is both an art and a medical practice based on terribly slow breathing exercises intended to balance the energy of the body and stimulate it in order to improve health, stave off disease and enable us to find harmony and serenity in life. I visited China in 1996 and spent several weeks in a massive sanatorium where patients with serious health conditions were treated for a month with nothing but qigong exercises from morning to evening. Following that visit, I was addicted to this amazing method and I immediately introduced it into my daily movement repertoire. About ten years ago, I also began to teach qigong once a week in a park not far from our home.

My practice of qigong also significantly improved my capabilities in other martial arts I trained in such as karate, Japanese Jujitsu and Japanese sword and stick training. That was why I decided to include several classic qigong exercises when I prepared the super-exercise training model. The beauty of the system is in its simplicity and minimalism. This method is based on slow movement, or even complete absence of movement. Unlike yoga, it does not push the joints of the body to their limits, and hence does not risk injury. Another way in which qigong contrasts with yoga is that it is performed solely on your feet, standing up. How can a method characterized by so little and such slow movement help us? This is, in my opinion, the best method developed by humanity to preserve and improve the function of our connective tissues.

The static postures and the slow stretching movements support the function of the connective tissues throughout our body and with it, the circulation of blood and lymph in the tissues. Qigong and tai chi have been extensively studied in medical literature and have been found to be highly effective in aiding patients with Parkinson's disease and preventing falls in the third age. According to traditional teachings, improvement, and progress in understanding the spirit of the method requires daily training of at least an hour solely in qigong. However, in spite of the benefits of this venerable tradition, few people can commit to such a dedicated training throughout their lives. As a result, the method never became as popular in the West as yoga. Nonetheless, qigong exercises meet all the criteria of classic super-exercises: they place minimal stress on the joints and so are completely safe; they are simple to execute, easy to learn, and can be performed at any age.

Here are a few examples of qigong exercises:

THE FEET IN QIGONG EXERCISES ARE PLACED USUALLY AT SHOULDER WIDTH AND ARE PARALLEL TO ONE ANOTHER.

- **Tree exercise**

This is the first and most basic exercise taught to me by Master Fong Ha: A simple stand. Breathe naturally, stand comfortably and continue standing. To the external observer this exercise may seem like the antithesis of physical activity or fitness but maintaining this posture for thirty minutes to an hour has incredible advantages. The entire body becomes relaxed and yet attentive, and the chi, that mysterious life energy, begins to flow and circulate throughout the body. **Furthermore, the body becomes whole and unified. This inner feeling supports us in any activity. When our body is properly and perfectly aligned, the nervous system can operate at its peak level, granting us a balanced and flowing movement.**

- **Shoulder delight exercise**

We move three areas of the body in this exercise, one after the other. First the knees perform a slight dip and then straighten up so the body stands up straight. Then the shoulders rotate either forward or back. Last is the head, which deeply nods up and down. We initiate the exercise with our back slightly bent forward, looking at the floor (the cellphone-stare position). We straighten our knees and towards the end of that movement, we begin to rotate our shoulders. Towards the end of the rotation movement, we look up, and then conclude by looking back down and bending our knees. This exercise requires precise coordination and constitutes an introduction to a group of back exercises that exists solely in qigong and in no other training method.

These are the "wave" exercises. In these exercises, the body performs a longitudinal movement of a wave. Envision a rope laid out on the floor, and when you lift its end, you perform a rapid up-and-down movement and send a wave across its entire length. This is a special movement which, in a very simple manner, preserves the flexibility of the spinal cord and prevents muscle cramps and various back problems. Unlike other back exercises, in the wave exercises, the entire body participates in a precise, flowing and completely harmonic movement.

This exercise has many versions, and it is highly recommended you immerse yourself in it, understand it and practice it daily. Wave movements are a way to perform a movement that was initially intended for swimming. That is how fish move, via a wave movement in their spinal cords. In our exercises, we perform "dry land" movement similar to butterfly strokes or diving with flippers.

Shoulder delight exercise - an excellent fascia exercise

- **Mountain exercise**

Stand with straight legs and lift your arms, straight up and extended to the sides. Lift your hands above your head, and then lower them via the midline of your body, with your palms naturally turning to the ground. You can also interweave your fingers and bring your interwoven hands via the midline of your body to maximum stretching over your head, and then lower your hands from the sides.

This exercise is a simple antidote for prolonged sitting.

> After you rise from the chair rebound a little, and then perform the mountain exercise. Remember that every stretch can instantly become an isometric exercise. I like to contract my muscles tightly at the peak of the mountain stretch, when my hand are raised as far as I can reach.

 Mountain exercise in qigong

Another version of the mountain exercise is presented in the illustrations below:

3   2   1

11   10

14   13   12

A wide variety of additional qigong exercises, both my own and those of other trainers, can be found online in YouTube videos.

Dr. Michael Herling demonstrates home fitness super-exercises and qigong.

- **Hand dancing exercises**

In these exercises, we wave our hands lightly from side to side or from back to front. These exercises are traditionally practiced as warmup in the beginning of tai chi or qigong training. These exercises are excellent for preserving the range of motion of your shoulder joints. See exercise number six in the movie below.

 Hand dancing exercise

The qigong super-exercises include various stretching exercises. Stretching exercises are extremely popular, and numerous people perform them as warmup prior to physical activity and/or as post-activity release. Sometimes, they perform only stretching exercises, such as in yoga. I prefer to perform stretching exercises as part of a dynamic exercise, rather than as a goal in and of itself. Stretching tendons and joints to their maximum range usually weakens the muscles.

Consider, for instance, a man descending to a full split. The man is without a doubt very flexible but he is weak, almost paralyzed, once in the split position, unable to move his feet powerfully or protect himself, making it a very bad survival posture. On the other hand, if we continue the hand movements in the mountain exercise towards the floor, we achieve a dynamic stretching of the hamstrings (the backs of the thighs), accompanied with harmonic movement of the entire body, which imitates lifting something from the floor.

As a final note, the practice of qigong has mental-emotional and spiritual aspects. This type of slow practice opens the door to inner realms such as those achieved through mindfulness, prayer, loving kindness, and guided imagery. It enables us to start our physical workout, with all its sweat and muscle pumping, at a more subtle level. Meditating while slowly moving is a great spiritual exercise. We are maintaining calmness and serenity while at the same time cultivating our connective tissue and moving our energy.

3.7 SEVENTH CATEGORY - CLASSIC EXERCISES

Classic exercises are all time favorites that we are all familiar with. These exercises rightfully appear in physical education classes in schools and fitness classes for adults, and so many people frequently perform them.

I chose to highlight the best three classics - squats, deadlifts, and push-ups - but you can freely add additional classics like the plank, lunges, burpees and many more.

SQUAT

There is an endless variety of exercises in the world, but the squat deserves special mention, for everyone dealing with fitness unanimously agrees that this is an *excellent* exercise!!

Before diving into detail about the squat, it is worth noting that the squat is not, in fact, an exercise; it is simply one of the ways we can sit down. That is why, even if you do not perform the exercise as detailed below, simply crouching down in a squat-like position for a prolonged period of time is an excellent exercise in and of itself.

Have you ever watched how two or three-year-old kids sit down? They drop into a squat and play in this position without any guidance, and without any problems maintaining balance or posture or creaking joints. In contrast, quite a few adults who try to drop down to a squat will not be able to get up without the help of the paramedics. Those who cannot drop to a full squat should work day by day, slowly but persistently, until they can match the squat of children. Be patient. You have your whole life to daily practice this movement.

The primary advantages of squatting exercises include:

- Full squats stretch our hip joints, knees and our Achilles tendon across their full ranges.
- Squats optimally align the colon and the rectum to the way we are designed to void our intestines while squatting. Furthermore, squats are highly recommended for anyone suffering from hemorrhoids, constipation and anal fissures.
- Rising from squats activates the posterior chain muscles, meaning the hamstrings, the muscles in the buttocks, and the thigh adductors. We tend to neglect these posterior muscles since we cannot see them, and work primarily on the chest and arm muscles. But the posterior muscles are essential for good, steady movements, as well as for stabilizing the pelvis and the lower back and are therefore critical to prevent back injuries.

In the popular fitness book "Starting Strength," Mark Rippetoe (2005) presents over a full chapter on squats. This chapter, which took me a week to read (and I read quite quickly), contains a comprehensive analysis of the squat position in its natural form as well as when weight is added. Some of the most highly recommended squat exercises include:

- **Squat sitting**

Sit in the squat position for as long as possible during the day. Adopt this crouch not as an exercise but as an alternate way of sitting. This sitting is actually a crouch, with the feet remaining fully on the floor. To descend to this position, stand with legs spread out approximately at shoulder width, with toes pointed out at an angle of roughly 30 degrees, tilt your pelvis outwards, bend your knees and simply get down. Ensure that your heels touch the ground (the tendency for most of us is to raise our heels upwards). If you find it difficult to sit in a squat with your heels touching the ground, I recommend you perform gradual stretching exercises to stretch and flex your Achilles tendon and improve the movement range of your knees.

- **Achilles tendon extension exercise**

Stand at the edge of a stair, rise up on your tiptoes, and then drop down. Your ankle will drop below the level of your toe tips, thus flexing, stretching and slowly elongating its tendons.

If you find it difficult to descend to a squat or rise from it, you can grip a pole or bannister and descend to a squat while holding on to the support.

- **Deep Squat**

Stand with legs spread out slightly wider than your shoulders and tilt your toes outwards, at an angle of 15-30 degrees. Now imagine that you are sitting on a stool just behind you. Beginners can place an actual stool behind them and sit on it. The movement is very simple, but people who are not familiar with it and whose body is not balanced, strong, or flexible enough, may perform it incorrectly. It is important to ensure the knees do not pass the toe line and to keep them aligned with the ankles and the feet, especially during the descent. The back should be kept as straight as possible. One way of fully understanding the squat movement is to perform it when facing a wall a few centimeters from your nose. The wall will ensure that you descend down in a straight line, neither bending your back nor leaning forward.

Throughout the squat, focus on a single point straight before you, or alternately, on a line on the floor two meters or about 6½ feet away. Push your pelvis outwards and bend your knees until your hip joints are at knee level or slightly lower. Throughout the exercise, be careful to tighten and engage your abdominal muscles and keep your back straight. Ensure the center of gravity is on your heels.

As soon as you reach the bottom, rise back up by pushing your buttocks and knees upwards, until you return to your starting position.

- **Squats with weights**

For beginners who are interested in performing squats with bar weights or a kettlebell precisely and productively, it is recommended they make use of the services of a skilled trainer or instructor. This exercise is less intended for the third age, and is not therefore considered a pure super-exercise.

(One of my variations is to use my children as weights, either seating them on my shoulders, or carrying them in the fireman's lift on my shoulders.)

A weight can be simulated at home by placing a broomstick across your shoulder blades. Though the broomstick does not weigh much, using it presses the upper back and shoulder blades into an isometric exercise of their own, beyond the actual squat.

- **Squat with an upper or forward jump**

This exercise is also not for everyone. But for young people in their early decades, this is an excellent athletic exercise that immediately raises the pulse and trains every muscle in the body. Drop down to a squat and when you rise, do so with lightning speed, as you leap upwards or forwards (frog jump). Swing your arms backwards at the sides of your body as you descend and upwards or forwards when you leap in a rapid, explosive movement.

There are endless squat variants that one can explore and invent. Here are just two that I do a lot:

- **Slow isometric squat**

Descend very slowly and at the same time, very slowly punch forward with clenched fists. Contract every muscle you can in your arms as hard as you can while moving them slowly forward. Imagine you are trying to move an extremely heavy object. As you ascend, slowly cross your arms to your chest and then slowly push them to the sides, once again forcefully contracting every muscle you can.

- **Wave squat**

Descend slowly and extend your arms forward with your palms facing the sky. Rise from the squat slowly and bring your palms to gently touch the sides of your waist, then slowly continue the movement of the hands backward while thrusting your pelvis forward. At the end of the movement, your entire back is arched and fully extended, your head is tilted back and your eyes are gazing up at the sky

DEADLIFT

This is a weightlifting exercise in which you bend and lift a bar weight over your knees to strengthen your lower back. It is superb in developing your body while involving every muscle in the body. It is, however, often neglected by gym trainers. Utilizing two heavy kettlebells can also simulate this exercise and enable its performance at home.

How to perform the exercise:

Stand with legs spread out at shoulder width with the kettlebell weights at the sides of your feet. Tilt your pelvis backwards, causing your back to bend forward somewhat.

Grab a weight in each hand, with your back straight and your eyes locked forward. Then tilt your pelvis forward by using your stomach and buttocks muscles, and straighten to a straight posture. Repeat the exercise sequentially. The exercise can also be performed by lifting the weights up only to the knees and then immediately dropping the weights back to the ground.

Beginners are advised to perform this exercise following a brief instruction to maintain correct posture throughout.

Deadlift with one kettlebell

Deadlift with two kettlebells

PUSH-UPS

This is a familiar and excellent exercise. In all its versions — from the plank to hand-stand push-ups — it trains the body in the movement element known as the push. In its classic form, of course, it requires descending to the ground – which is enough to make it a rare dish in the day-to-day movement menu of 99% of the population. It is also not so easy to perform.

And yet, it is well worth your time to acquaint yourself with the various versions of this exercise, if only because it trains and strengthens the palms of your hands to bear the weight of your body. A fracture of the palm or of the radial or ulna bones near the palm is quite common, especially in teenagers and in the third age. When we fall, our reflex is to halt our fall with the palm of our hand. Practicing push-ups will help you train and toughen up this part of your body, and prevent these fractures as much as possible.

As with every exercise, it is, of course, worth varying. For example, vary the width between your hands, perform push-ups on your fingertips, or perform the plank on your elbows or on your palms.

A simple version can be used in the third age. This version is a high push-up, performed while leaning your palms on a fence, table, or kitchen sink, while your feet are on the ground.

 Push-up versions

1

2

1

2

Those with high athletic capability can perform one handed push-ups or use a cute toy called a "neuro-grip" which transforms a simple push-up into a very difficult exercise.

Exercises relying solely on body weight are the best way to strengthen the body. Remember what Olympic athletes can do with rings, hanging bars, parallel bars and on the ground - all those impressive exercises, working only with their body weight. Over the past few years, an underground method called Street Workout has begun to gain popularity. This method is a collection of bodyweight exercises performed on whatever is available in the urban environment, but mostly utilizing hanging bars and benches. Bodyweight training is, by definition, always more functional than any other training, simply because the entire body is engaged in these exercises.

A final note: The king of bodyweight exercises is the squat. The squat joins the rebounding and dead hang to create what I call the three non-negotiables. Simply put, these trio of exercises are the best possible combination when looking for anti-aging effect. These exercises are the only ones that are performed at exact 90 degrees from earth. They are top-bottom, bottom-top movements. Practicing them daily will help maintain our height and preserve our structural integrity for life. Over the years I've met individuals who practice only one of the trios, but on a daily basis. One patient did 100 squats a day and that's it. No other routine or exercises. He was strong, lean and healthy until his final year when, at 92, he suffered a stroke and passed away.

3.8 EIGHTH CATEGORY - FREE SPONTANEOUS MOVEMENT

Free spontaneous movement is pure childlike and animalistic movement. Our brain does not instruct our muscles to move according to a predetermined pattern of an "exercise," and no one corrects us for deviating from its precise instructions.

Children and animals both often perform spontaneous, purposeless movements.

A spontaneous movement can be, for example, flinging hands in different directions while operating the feet in other directions, or spontaneous movement of the pelvis without any clearly defined or obvious goal, without any framework. When the random movement is more organized, we call it dancing. Spontaneous movement or dancing is available to us at any age, any location, and any health situation short of a coma. Spontaneous movement will always be diverse and different from the previous movement. This movement is characterized by very low intensity, does not last very long and can also be performed with music. Most importantly – this is an anti-block movement. The mind is utterly liberated of any opinion, thought or myth, and is occupied with one thing and one thing only: inventing a new movement every moment. That is why this movement is such a classical super-exercise.

This invented movement can sometimes be odd to watch. That is why I do not necessarily recommend you break out in spontaneous dance in the office, or spontaneously fling your smartphone at your boss for that matter. On the other hand, when you are alone or with your spouse, and especially with children, releasing the occasional spontaneous movement is highly recommended. I play with my children a great deal in inventing odd movements and faces, and we occasionally perform a play reminiscent of Monty Python's "Ministry of Silly Walks."

To those with even the slightest attraction to dance, I suggest joining some kind of dancing class, folk dancing, ballroom dancing, whatever. This is a super-activity very appropriate to the third age given the diversity of movement and the operation of the mind while engaging in fun activity. Folk dancing also involves constant contact with other people, which adds an important social component as well as a soothing touch to the movement.

Spontaneous movement with a light kettlebell weight can also be performed, providing enjoyable movement for several seconds, alongside more laborious muscle work. Spontaneous movement or dancing also has considerable influence on our spirit and soul. Our mind is liberated from fixations, and movement becomes experiential and personal, which is more than can be said for a deadlift in the gym.

3.9 NINTH CATEGORY - BREATHING EXERCISES

Breathing exercises are extremely important. Their purpose is to improve lung capacity and respiratory efficiency and to strengthen the respiratory muscles, particularly the diaphragm. I like to envision our chest as an accordion. When we breathe, we expand and contract this accordion. Breathing exercises mean playing with every parameter of this musical instrument. We can play with the duration of inhalation, exhalation, and of holding our breath. We can breathe through the nose or through the mouth, we can play with the volume of air we inhale into our lungs and so forth.

- **Diaphragmatic breathing/stomach breathing**

In this type of breathing, the diaphragm rises up and down and the stomach goes in and out. In extremely deep diaphragmatic breathing, the chest rises slightly and moves forward. This is the way babies breathe, and this is our natural breathing at rest. In our culture, where most of us sit for long hours on chairs while leaning forward, the stomach is pressured and collapses into itself, and the diaphragm stops moving altogether and transfers command to the chest muscles. However, chest breathing is shallower and less efficient than diaphragmatic breathing. To realize this you can place one hand on the lower abdomen, and the other hand on the chest, and breathe deeply. Take note: which hand moves? I have performed this exercise with thousands of patients. Some of them get it wrong sometimes, for they are not "connected" to their body, and although the hand on the chest is clearly moving, they answer, "the lower hand."

Diaphragmatic breathing results in a strong diaphragm. A weak diaphragm is one of the primary causes of stomach reflux, and for the regurgitation of stomach contents into the thorax.

Deep diaphragmatic breathing results in stimulation of the vagus nerve. This nerve is part of the parasympathetic nervous system, which is responsible, amongst its many roles, for relaxing the body when it is at rest. Stimulation of the vagal system therefore results in immediate relaxation. Furthermore, a study recently published in the Science Journal (Yackle et al., 2017) found that during deep diaphragmatic breathing, specific nerve cells report to another complex, the locus coeruleus – and these in turn communicate with areas in the brain associated with the relaxation response. This is why I recommend you adopt the habit of always breathing with your diaphragm when you are at rest. In contrast, forget about your breathing during dynamic exercises, and let it be natural.

- **Inhalation and exhalation of air versus resistance**

Another important exercise to improve lung volume and strengthen your respiratory muscles is via inhalation and exhalation of air versus resistance. There are several ways in which this resistance can be generated. You can blow up a balloon, for example, which forces you to exert the abdominal and chest muscles and exhale air with great force. Another way to do this, which is especially useful in physical training, is power breathing, also known as snakelike respiration. Take a deep, slow breath of air and exhale with a hiss.

There are also instruments recommended for those suffering from respiratory illnesses, which can be used to inhale and exhale versus resistance.

My favorite exercise for inhalation/exhalation versus resistance, is playing the didgeridoo. This ancient wind instrument, made of wood, was developed by the native aborigines in Australia. Circular breathing into a long didgeridoo is an excellent and extremely soothing respiratory exercise.

- **Yoga breathing**

Yoga contains many interesting breathing techniques which are highly recommended. One such excellent exercise is blocking one nostril and breathing in and out of the other nostril several times, and then switching to the other nostril.

- **Deep breathing**

As aforementioned, an important part of the system is based on qigong super-exercises. In these exercises, breathing is synchronized to slow movements, mainly of the hands. I recommend varying every exercise by inhaling and exhaling as deeply and for as long as you can. Several such boundary-pushing breaths every day will ventilate the dark, neglected corners of your lungs and will furthermore naturally soothe your nervous system.

- **Wim Hof breathing technique**

This excellent breathing exercise is not suited for everyone and proper guidance is often needed. But once you understand it, it can become a good way to balance and support the nervous system. See one of wim hof's YouTube video clip for detailed instructions of this breathing method.

 Wim Hof breathing technique

- **Holding your breath**

We are the only land animal that has the ability to hold our breath. Sea mammals have it, too, and use it for long dives underwater. Holding our breath creates certain stress on the body once carbon dioxide levels start rising in our blood. This triggers a chain of events that makes us more resilient.

A simple breath-holding routine I perform daily is exhaling and holding my breath whenever I walk, and counting how many steps I can walk without breathing.

Box breathing: This is simply a killer exercise. You inhale at the count of four, hold your breath to the count of four, breath out to the count of four, and hold your breath again (with no air in the lung) to the count of four. The count can be three or five or six, as best suits you. This exercise activates the parasympathetic nervous system and has a strong relaxing effect. I usually do it in bed before going to sleep. I do it in the car especially if I am caught in a traffic jam

Final notes: Breathing exercises can be a game changer. They are subtle exercises as they do not produce muscular biceps or a six pack, but they do train and strengthen the most important muscle in the body which is the diaphragm. Having an efficient breath means that oxygen and other nutrients are properly supplied to the tissues of the body. This fundamental process can and should be cultivated throughout our life since our lungs tend to lose their volume and elasticity as we age. Breathing exercises (along with isometric exercises) are invisible. You can perform them anywhere, anytime, without anyone noticing since they are completely internal. Thus I recommend making a habit of performing them practically anywhere and anytime on a daily basis.

3.10 TENTH CATEGORY - ANIMAL EXERCISES

This often neglected category of exercises brings us face-to-face with the inconceivably wide variations of human motion. Since our muscular and skeletal system are so multi-dimensional, we can imitate the walking and movement styles of many animals. The simplest exercise is simply to puff up our bodies, as many animals do to threaten others or make an impression: puff out your chest and spread your arms upwards.

Another simple exercise is what I call the Gorilla: vigorously pound your chest and your entire body with lightly clenched fists. This is an excellent exercise to wake up and invigorate your blood circulation.

This exercise can be taken one or two steps further by vigorously pounding for several minutes, with your open palm, on your entire body.

Here are a few examples of animal walks:

- **Bear walk**

Walk on all four limbs, with your hand and leg on the same side moving together frontwards and backwards.

- **Monkey walk**

Walk on all four limbs, with your opposing leg and arm moving forward at the same time, and the other leg and arm moving backwards.

- **Chimpanzee walk**

Walk on all four limbs, taking short hops sideways.

If you feel like practicing other animal walks, you can find YouTube videos illustrating the frog walk, kangaroo walk, alligator walk, tiger walk and more. Animal walk exercises are not classical super-exercises because for some people they are too difficult. However, given that they are excellent for younger people, I saw fit to include them here. These are truly excellent exercises for people who are already fit and wish to diversify their movements. Each of these exercises can be performed at growing difficulty levels. Children in particular love these exercises, and this is an excellent shared familial activity.

One final note: Animal exercises are part of my recommendations to osteoporosis patients. These exercises strengthen our wrists because they involve actively using our hands as feet. Strong wrists are crucial when we fall down and try to block the fall with our hands. (Wrist fractures are very common due to our intuitive use of them to block a fall.) Furthermore, animal exercises put our body in an unfamiliar dynamic posture close to the ground thus training our nervous and muscular systems in innovative ways.

3.11 ELEVENTH CATEGORY - FACIAL EXERCISES

The fascinating story of Alexander Mikulin inspired me in writing this book. He was born in Russia in 1895, became a senior engineer, and designed the Soviet Union's first jet engines. He suffered a severe heart attack around the age of 50, leading him to take up medical studies. He developed an original method to delay aging and preserve vitality and clarity, based on exercises utilizing engineering principles. He invented, among other innovations, the vibro-gymnastics, which is similar to rebounding but is performed with heels hitting the floor and transmitting slight shocks to the body. Mikulin would also perform complex facial exercises every morning. In his 80-year-old picture he seems younger than when he was 50. He completed medical school at the age of 80(!), and published his book "Active Life" at the age of 82. He passed away at the age of 90.

For most of us, the facial muscles remain a part of the body that we do not train, unless we are actors or singers. Why is it important for all of us to train these muscles? This region contains one of the most important muscle systems in our body – the system that chews our food and knows how to raise our lips into a smile. This part of the body is also the first people see when they meet you: your face. There is a reason, after all, that Botox injections and facial plastic surgery are so popular, for over the years the face changes and contributes to an old, tired appearance. Facial exercises help preserve the facial muscles and keep skin supple and expressive. Those who fear that the exercises will result in wrinkles need not be concerned. Since they are performed for only a short period of time, and gently, they will not result in any wrinkles.

Facial exercises include:

- Gently move your neck from side to side, and up and down. These motions will gently stretch out your facial skin.
- Perform a gentle massage of your forehead using four fingers which meet the four fingers of the opposing hand, and gently pull your fingers apart from the midline of your forehead to the temples.
- Shut and close your eyes forcefully.
- Massage your scalp and ears and gently tap your face and the back of your neck. This action will immediately bump your vitality and energy levels up.
- You can find additional amusing clips on YouTube that will show you how actors train their facial muscles, and how yoga exercises for the face can be performed.

Smiling and laughter are the foundations of a joyful life. That is why I strongly recommend you exercise your facial muscles, even via artificial laughter and smiling every day. Quite a few studies have demonstrated that laughter and smile therapy can improve blood sugar metabolism, strengthen the immune system, and reduce stress.

Final note: I use the time I spend driving to work and back to exercise my facial muscles. The car is ideal for this type of exercises since I am alone and the only people that might see me are other drivers. They might think I am crazy and try to stay away from my car – but that is a classical win-win situation.

3.12 TWELFTH CATEGORY

WALKING

Other than a small portion of the population that suffers from significant disability or a severe illness, all of us walk every day. Many people choose to expand their daily walking into a structured physical activity. The exact structure is different from individual to individual of course; walking every day at the same time, several times a week, on a treadmill, and sometimes more challenging walks such as a trekking in nature.

Walking does not constitute, in and of itself, a super-exercise. It utilizes only a small fraction of our muscles. It also does not require the active participation of the brain. Nonetheless, as many studies point out, this is an excellent physical activity. It realizes our historical movement on the ground to gather food and relocate from one area to another, the movement for which our bodies were designed. The very movement and operation of the body, even at low intensity, accelerates our metabolism and circulates the blood and lymphatic fluid at greater intensity, thereby gifting the body with an invaluable circulation of oxygen and clearance of waste from its cells. Common sense indicates that if walking is so healthy, activity involving more physical capabilities should be even healthier.

Leaving the house is a wonderful opportunity to interact with nature, just like children and animals do. Regardless of how your walking program is structured, I recommend you incorporate as many varied movements in it as possible. Thus, by incorporating the super-exercise philosophy into your walk, you can both enjoy the walking itself and the training of additional movement components and the participation of your brain in the exercise.

Most people living in the city walk in block formations, or a straight line, whether on the treadmill, set rounds around the block, or a linear walk on the flat beach, all at a uniform pace and walking posture. Such a walk is monotonous and automatic, much like a soldier on a parade, and does not activate the brain in any way whatsoever.

However, if you have already made the effort to reserve up to an hour for walking, why not also work your brain out a little bit? Why not exit the block while walking?

The following is a list of a few possibilities to diversify and enrich your walking:

(*All exercises to be performed while walking*)

- Throw both hands up to your sides and return them through the midline of your body, much like the qigong mountain exercise.
- Interlace your palms and lift them up, connected through the midline of the body over your head, and then take several steps with your hands lifted over your head.
- Rotate your shoulders forward and backwards, moving both shoulders together. Afterwards, rotate each of your shoulders separately, first one and then the other.
- Walk quickly without losing your walking posture.
- Transition from walking to a slow run in tiny, light steps.
- Transition from walking to a light run.
- Transition from walking to skipping from foot to foot.
- Walk barefoot. (Be careful, please!)
- Combine breathing exercises with your walk: breathe according to

your pace and constantly change your count. For example, take a deep breath over four paces and exhale over eight paces, and then change the combination.

- Fling your arms up in the butterfly or crawl swimming stroke, in tandem with walking.
- Walk with your knees lifted high in an exaggerated pose. The athletes amongst you can lift your knees until they touch your shoulder.
- Perform a variety of isometric exercises. For example, clench your fists as strongly as you can for several seconds, or clench your stomach tightly as you walk.
- Extend your fists forward at the pace of your walk (shadow boxing).
- Massage your face and scalp as you walk.
- Perform varied facial exercises as you walk.
- Jump forward on one foot, and then jump on the other. Jumping sideways on one foot is recommended for athletes, as if to escape a speeding bike, and then jumping immediately in the other direction, slowly advancing forward.
- Walk backwards.
- Walk with arm or leg weights and lift your arms/legs vigorously.
- Walk with your eyes closed and count the number of steps you can maintain while doing this.
- Perform a wave motion while you walk.
- Incorporate jumps forward, as if in an imaginary hopscotch game. For example, perform two jumps forward on one leg, and then another jump with two legs spread, then jump and close your feet, and perform another jump on one foot, or any other combination.
- Transition from usual walking to some kind of animal walking.
- Walk a little on the curb or on a fence in order to train your balance.
- Stop your walk, jump for a minute, and then resume walking.

Other than incorporating various diverse exercises into your walk, you can also stop walking and perform any exercise which comes to mind. For example, you can stop near a branch or a hanging bar in a playground or a park and perform a dead hang.

If you stop near a bench, you can jump on it or us it to perform push-ups. You can mix up the exercises I've described here and/or any additional exercises – you are certainly free and encouraged to invent more – into an hour of walking, and make it more interesting and certainly more effective.

When you walk with active variation, as described, the brain immediately becomes involved in the movement, for it must recall the exercise and concentrate on performing it. When the exercises simulate a climbing environment, in which the hands and legs perform different movements in different directions and angles, much involvement by the brain is required to synchronize the four limbs, and then plan the next exercise. Walks which seemed identical to every previous walk you have ever performed are suddenly transformed into a new, constantly changing exercise. In addition to integrating these exercises, you can always vary the sterile walking routine by taking alternate routes, or walking without shoes – activities that immediately place the mind on alert. Nature walks, hiking, walking in the rain and more are all viable options.

RUNNING

Much like walking, running is also a natural and simple activity. Modern running is a classical "block" activity, linear, monotonous and repetitive movements all within blocks, all the way to an orthopedic surgeon.

But much like walking, running, too, can be easily diversified. First, I recommend to anyone who selects structured running as a primary physical activity to complete the work on his own body with power exercises and varied jumping, as well as isometric exercises.

Second, every runner must protect his body from the attrition of monotonous movement by developing stabilizing muscles in his feet and a strong and flexible back, in order to absorb the shock of blows from the ground that reach the head from the feet, with minimal damage. Professional marathon runners often seem anorectic; their upper body is very lean, without much muscle mass. Their perseverance and durability are certainly admirable, but their bodies are not!

Every runner must study the optimal running movements. I recommend two excellent methods. The first is called ChiRunning, and the second is the Dr. Mark Cucuzzella method to minimize running injury risks.

Here are a few examples of exercises you can integrate during your running, and so diversify and enrich it:

- Perform sprints while you run. The athletes amongst you can perform an all-out sprint. If your track has a hill, then sprint up the hill instead of just running up it.
- Run sideways instead of forward.
- Run while high-skipping upwards.
- Run while simulating a step-and-a-half dunk like a basketball player, but without a hoop or a basket. (And unfortunately, no seven-figure contract for the next season.)
- Imagine yourself as Rocky, the boxer, in his last training before the big fight, and shadow box as you run.
- Try running in a body of water.
- Run barefoot. This is running that you need to adapt to and do gradually, because the muscle array in your feet must be strengthened in order to run barefoot. You can use very flat shoes, meant to simulate barefoot running.

- Run with very large steps, like a triple-jump leap.
- Run and jump forward like a long jumper.
- Run like a football player, with kicks and leaps to the sides.
- Incorporate all of these exercises one after the other rapidly. This is a very intensive exercise which will drain your reserves of strength, especially if you devote 10-20 seconds to every exercise.
- Join an instructor-led running group. In spite of the "blockiness" of this recommendation, running exercises in groups are usually more diverse and contain changes in rhythm and various other exercises, and so are more preferable to monotonous running at the same pace.

SWIMMING

Water movement is highly recommended, because, as I explained, we were designed to move, hunt, and gather in a water environment as well as on the ground. One of the nice things about swimming is that we are closest to our animalistic nature when we swim, since we are almost completely naked and surrounded by water in all directions. The main problem for most people is availability and cost. For those who can make swimming a regular exercise, this is an excellent activity. For those among us who already swim as a structured, regular activity, here are a few recommendations in the spirit of the system:

- Dive at every opportunity you have. For total beginners and for people in the third age, it is recommended they start gradually, and then slowly increase the distance and the duration of the dive.
- Perform athletic jumps in the water. Bend down until your head is water height, and then leap upwards, just like whale or a dolphin leaping up and into the air. This is an excellent exercise, since it incorporates land-based athletic abilities in a water environment,

which completely buffer the shocks caused to the joints.

- Vary every parameter of swimming. Practice breathing exercises in the crawl. Breathe every four-to-five movements, incorporate between different numbers of breathing and more. I like breathing at every motion, and then every two motions, and then every three motions, then four, five, six, seven and eight motions – and then backwards

- Gradually try to swim the entire length of the pool without breathing.

- Try swimming with fins and diving with them like a dolphin.

- Swim sprints, even very short sprints of a few meters, but in an all-out style.

- Swim in a sea or an ocean. Swimming in the ocean constitutes, by definition, a diverse swim since the waves and currents constantly change the resistance of the water. We are also more vigilant when we swim in the ocean, as we are exposed to the sun and the chill of the water, enabling us to be in contact with the electromagnetic field of the planet. During the winter, the cold water adds another layer of stress and challenge that strengthens us.

3.13 THIRTEENTH CATEGORY - TRICKS AND ACCESSORIES

Look around you and note just how many human-made objects you are surrounded with: furniture, electric appliances, kitchenware, books, pictures, light fixtures, keys, clothing accessories, children's toys, cosmetics, and more and more. There are thousands of accessories in an average home. Why not add several items that will diversify your movement?

TRICKS AND TOYS

Here are several purposeful accessories that can easily be acquired:

- Pull up bar - an absolute must in every home.
- Medicine balls - in a variety of weights starting with a 1-kilo-weight softball (2.2 lb) that you can catch in one hand. There are infinite exercises that can be performed with a medicine ball. It is superb for practicing any qigong movement or stretching exercise, and enables training of your grip during training. A medicine ball can also be used to juggle by throwing from hand to hand, or playing catch with your children or spouse. You can also perform push-ups with your hands gripping a medicine ball or two, or try to stand on a medicine ball with either one or both legs.
- Hanging rings - such as TRX or the like. Working with rings is an excellent exercise and subject to infinite variation.
- A small, medium or large trampoline.
- Indo board - this is an elliptical wooden board placed on a rigid cylinder which was originally developed for surfers. It has turned out to be an excellent training tool for the land as well, for it activates the core muscles and improves balance and coordination.
- T-shaped neuro grips for push-ups - these are a more challenging sort of push-up handle and they are a particularly challenging accessory suitable for athletes who want to push their limits.
- Jump rope.
- Juggling accessories - such as juggling balls, poi balls (a tethered-weight ball with Maori origins) or a slack-line (flat webbing which stretches between two anchors for ultimate balance exercises).
- Leg and arm weights - these are placed on the ankles or the hands and then put out of one's mind. Once we strap these weights on,

we can walk about our daily routine at home with a few additional weight percentage points on us without even thinking about it.

- A broom stick and a short stick - there are a variety of flexibility exercises that can be performed with a stick. They can be used to practice martial arts movements, and batting movements similar to baseball.
- Punching bag - there is nothing like an old-fashioned punching bag for a short speed-training session to unwind and aid in stress relief.
- Martial arts accessories - boxing gloves, sticks in a variety of lengths, swords, nunchaku and more. There is no need to actually practice martial arts in order to play with swords and sticks. You just need to be very careful if you are untrained, in order to avoid harming yourselves or those near you.

Two tricks that I like to add to almost every exercise are training with eyes closed and training on one leg. First, try standing on one leg with your eyes closed. Any super-exercise, except of course for those on pull-up bars, can be performed on a single leg. If you can perform a one handed pull-up, that is a sign that you are super-fit.

Any exercise can be performed with closed eyes. This immediately and automatically sharpens your other senses. Physical movement with closed eyes immediately recruits more brain cells; when your eyes are closed, your brain signals the moving body that it must be alert. The body tenses up a bit, and movement becomes slower. The brain opens up all other information channels to compensate for loss of sight, especially when we move our legs.

Try jumping with your eyes shut, lifting a kettlebell with eyes shut, or standing on one leg with your eyes shut. Try performing qigong exercises like the mountain while standing on one leg with your eyes closed. This exercise can challenge anyone who performs it, even someone in peak condition. This is an excellent exercise for the foot- and ankle-stabilizing muscles, and for maintaining a strong, steady ankle.

3.14 FOURTEENTH CATEGORY - FASCIA EXERCISES

This series of exercises is unique to the SET method, and they conclude the super-exercises series.

The fascia is a thin casing of connective tissue that surrounds and holds every organ, blood vessel, bone, nerve fiber and muscle in place. Given what I have learned about the fascia and its role in movement, I believe that the series of exercises dedicated to it is essential to the preservation of the capabilities of our bodies and of smooth, painless movement throughout our lives. This series of fascia exercises has four components, three of which are also associated with other groups we have studied about:

- Slow stretches - our fascia loves slow stretches of the entire body. Basic stretches such as bending down to the floor with our hands, stretching upwards, or various yoga positions leads the fascia to expand and contract and enables it to receive fresh blood supply. That is why hanging bar exercises or qigong stretching exercises are ideal and should be repeated several times each day.
- Rebounding - fascia tissue is elastic and in order to maintain its elastic springlike quality, it is recommended you perform spring-like, elastic, rapid rebounds on a daily basis. (Details of these exercises can be found in Category 3.1.)

The rebound is an ideal power exercise for the entire body. As time goes by, you should aim slowly to increase the height, spring, and power in your jumps. It is enough to jump two-to-four high, powerful jumps once a day. For those who have not jumped in many years, it is recommended you start with light jumps in place, with only a slight lifting of the heel. A study published in 2015 in the European Journal of Applied Physiology examined the impact of rebounding exercises on the fascia tissue of 20 elderly participants. The researchers discovered considerable improvement in many parameters, such as jumping height, Achilles tendon quality, ankle joint quality, and more.

- Perfect posture - fascia tissue flourishes when the entire body is in a perfect posture, free of pain and stress. The qigong standing exercise, a simple exercise performed for several breaths while arranging the body into an aligned, stress-free posture, improves the function of the connective tissue throughout the body.
- Gentle massage - our fascia tissue loves gentle, non-painful massage. Regular massages are highly recommended for those who can afford it and who are not averse to the touch of strangers. I prefer to use several accessories as substitutes for the classic massage. A long foam roller and several small balls are all that is required to gently massage the body. There are several ways to work with a foam roller. Of all of the methods I examined, I particularly enjoy a system called the "melt system." This is gentle, painless work which can easily be incorporated into your daily activity. For example, while you are sitting at work or at home, roll a small ball beneath your foot and massage it. The gentle massage encourages the hydration of the fascia tissue, encouraging its flexibility and reduces pain and stress. It takes time to learn how to work correctly with the foam roller, but the result is certainly worth the investment. We become our own masseuse, available, free of charge, and always compassionate and attentive.

It is recommended to perform the fascia exercises throughout the day, and there is no need to do them all at once. For the fascia exercise see the movie link below.

 Fascia exercise – stretching, rebounding, posture, foam roller

A PERSONAL EXAMPLE FOR INCORPORATING SUPER-EXERCISES IN A TYPICAL WEEK:

Morning:-The house wakes up. The bleary-eyed children begin wandering and gathering their strength for the morning grumbling. Moans and loud yawns can be heard from the parent's bedroom. Another day begins – a day in which I juggle four children, work in a packed clinic, and accomplish the other daily chores.

On the way back from the restroom, I start my super-exercises by hanging on a bar for several seconds, and then I usually perform another exercise, such as two pull-ups or isometric hanging on a pull-up bar (15-20 seconds). Immediately thereafter, I rebound several times (10 seconds or 20 jumps). Then I am sucked up by the natural vacuum of the morning tasks. For a few seconds, I will put one of my children on my shoulders and perform deep squats, and then I will pack the kids up, "express mail" them to their educational routines and head off for work.

I descend the stairs to the yard and immediately come face-to-face with the pull-up bar I have set up there. Straps, Olympic Rings and TRX are hanging on the bar, and two kettlebells lie besides them. First, I perform an upside-down hang. Sometimes, I will perform five sit-ups from this upside-down hang position, and sometimes I will perform some other combination of hanging exercises. I very much like to catch the TRX straps and perform full rolls forward and backwards (60-120 seconds). After that, I perform weight exercises with the kettlebells (30 seconds), do some more rebounding and conclude with several qigong exercises facing the sun (60-90 seconds), after which I will pound my chest like a gorilla (10 seconds) and head off to work.

I have four streetlights to pass on my way to work. As I invariably sit at one of them, I perform an isometric exercise in the car, as if I am trying to crush the steering wheel or rip it out of place (five seconds).

I have a hanging bar, two kettlebells and one medicine ball in my clinic. I explain the training method to two-to-three patients a day, which means demonstrating exercises. That means I get to rebound (20 seconds or 40 jumps) and work with my kettlebells (30 seconds). During my morning shift alone, I end up hanging on the bar two or three times (15 seconds).

Twice a week I do not have afternoon hours at the clinic, which usually means I will take some combination of children to the playground nearby. Believe me, I know this territory like the back of my hand. I have preset stations in the playground. I climb two trees (each for 10-20 seconds), hang and play on a variety of beams. I use the swings and beams for balance exercises, and try to walk along the fence surrounding the garden. Sometimes I take a skateboard and ride it as the kids horse around in the garden, while the weary eyes of the other parents are fixated on the screen of their smartphones.

There is almost always activity with the children over the weekends, and wherever it occurs – in the ocean, the park or the garden – I find that is the time and place to move your body. I jump with several children on the big trampoline, usually for half-an-hour of random jumping, rolls and tickling. Occasionally, I also jump on my own in the big trampoline (120 seconds).

In the evening, at home, I perform additional squats and rebounds, practice with a sword or a stick, juggle a little, perform animal walking, pull-bar exercises, and various other stretching and qigong exercises, in a random and spontaneous order. I integrated the exercises with the various other tasks of the evening (a total of about five minutes) several times a week, during the evening I will give myself massage with the foam roller (2 minutes). I frequently speak with my wife during the stretching and isometric exercises. (Fortunately, she is used to it.) I also try to play on the piano and didgeridoo for several minutes each day.

It is very difficult for me to assess the total time of my evening exercises since my schedule constantly changes. But although it looks like a long workout, it is, in fact, only about five or ten minutes scattered between many exercises and games. To sum up my activity throughout a typical day, I perform super-exercises for about half-an-hour, including my time with my children. If you knock off the time I spend with the kids, I work out only 10-15 minutes a day. Notice that the exercises stretch from morning to evening, and are made up of at least 12-13 intervals, and another 10-20 intervals of a single movement or stretch. From morning to evening, I train all muscles in my body, and all movement components in such a way that no day is like the one preceding or succeeding it. All this is done at extremely low intensity, given the extremely brief training period. But any exercise can be made very difficult within no more than ten seconds, so that I flirt with my comfort zone here and there, but never too much.

This entire training occurs in my home and work environment, without reserving any time for it or changing clothing to do it. I do not use pulse-measuring gadgets or any advanced gym instrument, I do not tire myself out, and I do not wear down my joints with extended activity or special exertions.

I like to constantly check out new exercises, new methods and new training gadgets.

I usually reserve the all-out exercises for my sports hobbies, but I do challenge my comfort zone several times a day, especially with isometric exercises and animal walking. I almost never practice until reaching muscle failure, for the simple reason that I do not want my muscles to learn to fail. I will note that you should never train to the point of muscle failure; working at half your capacity is enough if you do so daily. That is the training method of weightlifters from the ex-Soviet Union who dominate the field. They train daily but at a low intensity.

We have reviewed 14 categories of super-exercises: jumps, hanging, kettlebell, isometric exercises, qigong exercises, classic exercises, free movement, breathing exercises, facial exercises, animal walks, all-out exercises, walking/ running/ swimming, tricks/accessories and fascia/ connective tissue exercises.

Before diving into the how-to of practically implementing the system into our daily lives, let me reiterate the fundamental principles of SET:

PRINCIPLE #1

Holistic approach - SET is designed for everybody no matter what age, gender, health status, income etc.

SET can be practiced anywhere and anytime making it totally independent of time, place, weather, availability, and Corona restrictions.

SET holistically trains all the seven components of physical activity; strength, agility, balance, etc.

PRINCIPLE #2

The best possible approach - SET selects and emphasizes the best exercises ever created. They are called super-exercises. These exercises must meet the following strict criteria: they must be easy to learn; they must be simple to do; they must keep one completely safe from injuries; they must be able to be done according to my first principle, which is "by everybody, anytime, anywhere."

PRINCIPLE #3

Super-freedom - SET inspires us to move like animals or children, hence the mantra "every day, all day, all your lives, anywhere, every which way." In SET, we become our own trainer and we own and are fully in charge of our movement, thus creating total freedom of choice and enabling us to reacquire child-like and animalistic fitness.

PRINCIPLE #4

Anti-aging - SET is designed to ensure graceful aging. A primary goal of the system is that it helps to preserve and cultivate our overall fitness throughout our life cycle, especially as we age.

How can we possibly cope with so many exercises and versions? It is precisely the variety of the system which enables us to learn to "speak" the language of movement. To speak a language well, any language, we must learn to speak many words and learn how to use them in different combinations. Ultimately, the test of whether we are truly fluent in the language is if we can joke in it. The exercises selected here are mostly simple, readily available, and easy to perform. And so, you can begin to learn the language immediately, on this very day, and continue to learn to practice it over your entire life. The constant learning, variety and innovation will enable you to continue with it throughout your entire life without growing bored, being injured or investing too much time in it.

Once you learn the exercises presented in this book, and perhaps from YouTube as well, you will prepare a bank of your favorite exercises. And it shouldn't take too long, either, a few weeks to a couple months maybe. I recommend you diversify your exercises as much as possible, and occasionally also perform an exercise you are less fond of. The period allotted to each exercise is so short, after all. The nature of the exercises, their order, intensity, and period of time in which you perform them, and the hour of the day is all spontaneously determined by you. After several months, once your body grows stronger (or immediately for those in top shape), I recommend you constantly vary each of the basic exercises. Every brief rebounding session should be a bit different than the one preceding and succeeding it: in one set you will jump 9 seconds, and in another you will jump 20 seconds; in one session, you will jump very low, and in the other very high; one day you will open and close your legs, and the next day, you will jump on one foot.

You will discover after a few months that your entire day is intertwined with brief stretches of good movement. At this stage, the animalistic intuition of your body will have been awakened, and with it also the joy of movement and play. Slowly, you will begin to see how you can perform more exercise intervals and incorporate them in everything you do, by constantly using your environment as a playground.

All of these basic exercises can be learned alone, and easily, in the comfort of your home. As I constantly reiterate throughout this chapter: anyone, of any age, can learn to perform them. There is no time pressure whatsoever, for these exercises will accompany you throughout your life. That is why you can study them at your own pace and utilize them joyfully.

So how do you get started?

First, you need to make time. Get up ten seconds earlier in the morning or move meetings and somehow clear up ten seconds during your workday. In the first ten seconds of your training in this method, select one of the super-exercises from the fourteen categories presented here. In the days, weeks, months, and years that follow, commit yourself to train for at least ten seconds every day. Gradually, at your own personal pace, add more ten-second segments. These segments can lengthen an exercise you are already performing from ten seconds to twenty or thirty seconds, or for any duration of time you wish. You can also practice these segments later in the day. The training time during the day can change, as can the length and nature of each exercise. Thus, the mantra of the super-exercise method can be implemented on the very first day:

"Every day, all day, every which way, for your entire life."

The three non-negotiables (rebounding, hanging and squatting) are an excellent starting point. Perform them throughout your day, spontaneously, for several seconds each. They can be performed in a single session of 30-60 seconds or done separately. The emphasis should be on doing the exercises **every day**.

If you cannot easily squat, you can skip this exercise and come back to it when you feel ready. Learn a new exercise at your own pace by coming to this book, and immediately try to incorporate it into your daily movement. I suggest starting with breathing exercises and the fascia groups of exercises. These groups of anti-aging exercises are soft, gentle and can be easily practiced daily.

As the weeks and month pass by, you will slowly learn how to be your own master. Like a child or an animal, you will be in full control over your own movement pattern — no rules, no time frames, no right or wrong. This freedom of movement matched with the best exercises ever done will have a tremendous effect on your body and mind. You will slowly become stronger and more in tune with your body.

Here are a few suggestions of a daily routine you can follow:

- 07:00 - Hang from a bar for five seconds
- 07:15 - Rebound for ten seconds
- 07:30 - Shoulder movement exercise from the qigong exercise group-1-5 reps
- 08:30 - All-out isometric exercise performed in your car by trying to crush the steering wheel with your hands, followed by face exercises
- 13:00 - The qigong mountain exercise, 1-5 reps
- 20:00 - Foam roller massage
- 20:05 - Hang on a bar for five seconds
- 20:05 - After hanging on the bar, stand in a steady, erect posture without moving, and perform two box breaths for about 30 seconds
- 20:30 - Squat in front of the television for 20 seconds

The exercises described above will take up a few minutes every day, depending on the time you devote to the foam roller. The times at which you perform the exercises is dependent solely on our choice and can be completely random. They can also of course be concentrated, in the morning or evening, or any other hour you might choose. You can also decide to focus on a single group of exercises, such as hanging on a bar or rebounding, and develop only this group. Start with jumping 10 seconds a day, reach 20 seconds a day after a month, 30 seconds a day of varied rebounding after three months, jump six 10-second intervals a day after a year, and a year thereafter, progress to a trampoline 5-10 minutes per day, or use a jump rope for 2-3 minutes every day. Alternately, you can hang on a bar for about 5 seconds a day, move on to 10 seconds four times a day after two months, a half-minute of consecutive hanging after a year, and two years later you may begin performing a single pull-up. Older people and individuals without basic fitness or physical awareness must progress very slowly and avoid excessive enthusiasm. Remember: this is training for your entire life, and our exertion scale stretches from this day to our last. That is why it is recommended to increase the training volume slowly, while listening to your body. I told one of my patients, 89-year-old A., the story of Alexander Mikulin (see 3.11), and the great benefits of rebounding. I taught him about medical rebounds in my clinic and instructed him to jump 10-20 seconds every day and add a 10-second interval every few weeks.

At our next meeting I asked A. how he was doing, and he told me that he was so excited with the rebounds, and simply being able to jump, that he began to jump every day, all day. However, he soon began experiencing knee pains which stopped once he ceased jumping. I reemphasized to him the importance of gradualism and a slow but steady exertion scale.

Here is an example of a daily exercise routine for an individual with reasonable basic fitness:

- Three-to-four jumping intervals of 10-30 seconds each
- Hanging on a bar 3-4 times a day for 5-10 seconds each time
- Several stretching exercises from the qigong group throughout the day
- Half-a-minute of kettlebell play
- Several isometric exercises in your car when stopped at a red light
- Several push-ups
- A rapid sprint in place
- Squat crouching for several seconds followed by 10 simple squats
- Several facial exercises while driving a car or sitting on the toilet
- Listening to a favorite song and dancing freely to it

- Foam roller massage
- Taking 10 deep breaths before going to sleep, with the exhalation longer than the inhalation

Thus, for 4-5 minutes scattered throughout the day, we visit all movement components in a varied manner.

Here is an example of a more intensive and more diverse exercise regimen:

- Skipping rope for 200 consecutive jumps
- Performing a Wim Hof breathing exercise followed by 50 push-ups
- Five slow pull-ups
- Five athletic rebounds
- Ten stretches on the hanging bar throughout the day
- Qigong exercises scattered throughout the day, with emphasis on breathing as deeply as possible
- Ten 16-kilo (~34 lb) kettlebell Russian swings
- Twenty behind-the-back kettlebell passes in each direction
- Isometric exercises throughout the day, with one of them being a half-way pull-up on a hanging bar, and remaining there for 30 seconds until the hands begin to shake
- Swimming and diving in the ocean

Note again that each of these exercises can be infinitely varied by changing the duration of the exercises, increasing or reducing the number of repetitions, performing the exercise faster or slower, performing the exercises in a different order or spacing, or replacing one intensive exercise such as the Russian swing with another intensive exercise such as the isometric towel exercise or another intensive kettlebell exercise.

One can take a single group of exercises and practice that set, and that set only, for 10 minutes; for example, 10 minutes of varied rebounds on a trampoline or 10 minutes of body weight training such as a hanging bar combined with diverse push-ups or 10-minutes of pure kettlebell training.

My recommendation is to spread out all these exercises throughout the day. They can, however, also be performed in sequence, and varied. Once you've established your daily habit, your emphasis should then be in favor of innovation and novelty. Once in a while, come back to the book and learn something new or improvise and invent some new sequence. This way you can fully enjoy all the health benefits of movement.

In the following video clips I demonstrate two simple short sequences of basic super-exercises. The duration of each sequence is roughly two minutes. In each sequence, I perform the following exercises –hanging, rebounding, squatting, qi qong stretches and shoulder rolls, isometrics and breathing exercises like box breathing and slow deep breaths. In the first sequence I preform the exercises in a simple, comfort zone way with no variations. In the second sequence I show how to infuse the same basic exercises with variations and athleticism.

First sequence

Second sequence

Some people find it difficult to be their own masters of movement after years of "block" movement and being used to getting specific orders and instructions from trainers. Some people I've met are less attracted to this concept of freedom and constant learning and changing. That is perfectly fine. I have a 63-year-old patient who is doing 200 push-ups a day and running 2-3 times a week and playing the flute daily. Remember, too, the 92-year-old who only did squats every day, but did 100 repetitions. Once you are doing the best exercises on a daily basis, that is good enough.

Over a number of months and years you can sample, develop, improve, and deepen each of the exercise categories. Thus, your training might one day look like this:

- One hundred diverse jumps in the morning
- Ten hanging-bar stretches throughout the day
- Riding a bicycle to a park with fitness instruments, and performing body-weight exercises and plyometric rebounds for 10 minutes
- Fascia tissue exercises
- Facial and isometric exercises randomly embedded throughout your day

- Juggling with three balls
- Qigong exercises like dancing hands and shoulder movements embedded throughout the day
- Crouching for several minutes in the squat position in the evening

The next day your training might look like this:

- Pilates/yoga/running in the morning
- Ten stretches on the hanging bar throughout the day
- Climbing trees or various playground facilities with the children
- Twenty varied push-ups, eight varied squats
- A single minute of play with a medicine ball with your spouse
- Five minutes of foam roller massage
- Breath-holds while walking and 10 box breaths before sleep

The following day, your training might look like this:

- Five minutes jumping on a trampoline
- Seeking personal record in an isometric exercise of hanging on a bar without moving
- Trying an upside-down hang for the first time in your life
- Several simple stretches throughout the day

In this way, it is possible to continue to vary your daily practice of SET so that every day will be different from the day preceding it and the day following it. Every day we visit at least three-to-four groups of exercises, frequently even more. So the training progresses over the years, until you know many exercises and many variants of those exercises. At that point, the training flows spontaneously and intuitively, with you pushing and releasing the intensity pedal in accordance with your needs, goals and lifestyle. By daily practicing a variety of super-exercises, your body adopts and slowly but surely you come to perform them better and better. That is the best way I know for preserving those exercises for life.

As you can see, the possible combinations are almost endless. But the beauty of it is that we have our entire life to explore it. And moreover, everybody can do it.

In the next chapter, we will revisit the exercise groups through the lens of the basic components of movement

CHAPTER 4

Super-Exercise Training for Each of the Movement Components

As I explained in Chapter 2, one of the central themes underlying the super-exercise training model is the importance of practicing all the components of movement every day: speed, strength, flexibility, balance, coordination, endurance, posture. In the current chapter, I will expand on each of these components and explain which exercises will train each component. Super-exercise training enables us to train all the components of movement spontaneously and very briefly throughout the day, thereby putting less stress on the body. When you train all movement components spontaneously and unexpectedly every day, your body will learn how to adapt to the change and will become supple, strong and energetic.

4.1 STRENGTH

Strength is the most important of all the activity components, and its importance only increases the older we get. In ancient times, physical strength is what determined how much one ate and whether one would survive, and it remains of supreme importance to the present day. It determines how we will function in the new environment we have created over the past century. A weak person is not as happy as he could be if he were stronger. I do not intend by these words to dismiss the intellectual or spiritual aspects of life, of course, but rather to emphasize that even those individuals who highly prioritize these aspects in their lives will feel better and be healthier and happier when they train and strengthen their body.

Modern developments have released most of us from the need to operate our body to secure basic needs such as water, food, shelter, clothing and medication. Thus, most physical activity today is purely a matter of choice. Even if the purpose of physical activity is no longer immediate survival, it is still essential to preserving physical and mental health, and its stimulus shapes our entire body including the brain. If we are not careful to perform some level of physical activity, various health complications are sure to emerge.

That said, why is strength is the most important of the seven components of physical activity?

Muscle strength underlies each and every movement, for physical activity is performed by definition by movement and contraction of the muscles. We also often confuse sport with physical activity. Physical activity is any motion we perform to achieve a particular goal in the physical world around us — such as getting a jar from the shelf, lifting up a crate, going shopping or rising from the floor. In contrast, sport is a hobby whose goal has no immediate link to a vital functional activity in our environment.

It is very important to understand that a sports hobby trains the body to excel in the hobby itself and no more. An individual who practices running will only be good at running. When this long distance runner rides a bike or plays basketball, he will be no more capable than any other beginning cyclist or novice basketball player. A man who practices yoga will only be good at yoga, and a swimmer will only excel in swimming.

In contrast, an individual who performs basic strength exercises will enjoy an advantage in any physical activity he may perform. That is why these exercises are good for everybody regardless of whether they are professional athletes or amateurs, whether their main hobby is walking on the treadmill, or whether they are in their eighth decade of life and just now want to begin training.

In the third age, muscle mass begins to atrophy as part of the irritating aging mechanism called sarcopenia or muscle loss. At the same time, other systems deteriorate and a marked social and professional decline occurs. Of all the irritating aging processes, sarcopenia is the only one against we can take action. How? Via exercises that strengthen the body. In the third age, it is our body strength that determines the strength of the bone, our ability to lift weights such as our grandchildren, or our ability to rise from the chair. Correct use of muscle mass will determine metabolism, and for men, their testosterone levels. Many studies demonstrate that strength training greatly improves our health, especially in the third age. (See for example: Barbieri, E. 2015; Carter, Chen & Hood, 2015; and Johnson, Robinson & Nair, 2013.)

Strengthening the body is also the primary antidote to the general degeneration so prevalent in our modern, seat-stuck society. It is also the easiest target to achieve, with the most rapid progress. Our muscles should work against resistance; that is what they do all the time. The muscle does not care if the weight is the body weight or the external weight of a kettlebell. Basic strength exercises, with proper instruction, also contain the components of good posture, flexibility and endurance.

Muscles grow stronger only when they are stimulated into strenuous action. We know that the activity really is strenuous when the muscle tires, fails, and aches. This is a major obstacle for most people, who quite reasonably see no advantage in feeling muscles burn or have no motivation to lift heavy objects or feel any sort of effort. Of course, life itself may occasionally require us to invest in efforts such as carrying bags from the supermarket, moving a heavy table, lifting children and grandchildren. In these cases, we summon the motivation because it is a necessity.

There are no weights or gadgets in nature but nevertheless, animals have excellent fitness from the day they are born until the day they die. This indicates that natural muscle strengthening is primarily based on body-weight exercises. Accessories can certainly be helpful; hand weights, bar weights, elastic bands, straps, TRX, medicine balls – all are good. Of these, I personally selected isometric exercises and kettlebell weights. What distinguishes isometric and kettlebell exercises from the rest is their great diversity. This is in direct contrast to the exercises people do in the gym, which tend to repeat again and again until most people get terribly bored. In spite of the great importance of strength exercises, unfortunately its value and significance are often insufficiently emphasized.

Below are several highly recommended strength exercises:

- Isometric exercises - as I noted in the previous chapter, these are the simplest and most efficient exercises to strengthen the muscles.
- The squat - this excellent exercise (see performance instructions in Chapter 3), when performed correctly, is the best exercise to activate the posterior chain muscles, specifically the hamstrings, the buttock and the thigh adductor muscles. In fact, no single exercise can train all these muscles at once across the entire range of motion of the thighs.

These muscles are the most important muscles for the movement and strength of the entire body. When the squat is performed with weights on one's shoulders, it becomes the best strength exercise possible, for it strengthens almost all the muscles of the body as you move. This includes the core muscles, the innermost muscles of the abdomen and back, that stabilize the body and assist in its movement. The squat also maintains the important movement ranges of the thighs, knees, and ankles. The exercise is safest when it is performed in correct posture and enables a rapid rise in strength.

I recommend you practice it once or twice a week with weights or a stick. People with impaired movement range of their thighs and/or knees, whether due to lack of training or advanced age, can replace this exercise by pushing weights with a leg press.

You can add also elements of a squat into rebounding by descending halfway down into a squat and then leaping high. This is a rather hard exercise to perform, but it is highly recommended for those who wish to improve their athletic capabilities. I very much suggest that you make the effort and learn how to perform the squat correctly and perform several squats every day, if only to preserve the range of motion of your thighs and knees, and if you perform the squat fully, all the way to the bottom– also the proper length of the Achilles tendon.

- Another excellent variant of the basic squat is to descend all the way down to a squat until the buttocks almost touch the floor, with your hands placed on one another as in an Indian blessing, and use the elbows to push your knees to the sides so that your legs are slightly spread out. It is worth remembering that the squat position is also the position that nature intended for us to defecate in. In this position, the terminus of the digestive tract is at an angle that enables optimal passage of the feces. One reason for the high frequency of hemorrhoids and anal fissures is due to the way we sit on toilet seats, which is completely unnatural. A simple way to fix this is by placing your feet on a low stool in front of the toilet seat. The squat is also highly recommended as a seating position, along with cross-legged sitting and the Japanese Seiza. (Seiza translates to sitting with a correct posture, the formal way to sit on Japanese floors.) Children naturally crouch down in a squat and only later on, when they get used to sitting on a chair by a table, do they slowly lose the ability to remain in this posture. The shortening of the Achilles tendon, caused by prolonged sitting on chairs, prevents contact of the heel with the ground, and hence we lose the ability to lower our buttocks all the way down to the end of our movement range. The squat is such a good exercise, that it is enough to perform it 50-100 times per day in several varieties as your sole activity. Daily practice of it will strengthen every muscle in your body! As in many strength and power exercises, I recommend contracting the abdominal and back muscles as much as possible by emitting a hissing sound when you exhale, and by constantly maintaining awareness of your abdominal area and keeping it engaged in the exercise. In the squat, for example, when we rise, it is important to emphasize not only the contraction of the thigh muscles, but also the contraction of the abdominal muscles. You will discover that the movement is much easier and safer when it is performed with clenched stomach muscles, even though the thighs continue to contract.

- Deadlift - lifting weights to waist level (see instructions in Chapter 3). This is a classic gym exercise. Although this is not a simple exercise and it is important to perform it with proper posture and with the aid of an instructor for beginners, there is no better exercise to strengthen the muscles of the lower back. The ability to keep a stiff lower back is critical for the transfer of strength from the legs to the upper body. The lower back muscles operate isometrically, which means they contract without creating a movement, but only to hold the spinal cord in place. Strong back muscles are a must for good back health. The overwhelming majority of lower back injuries are caused by weak, unbalanced muscles.

- Push-ups are how you practice the press using the bodyweight alone. Various versions of push-ups are excellent exercises in and of themselves that train most muscles of the body. Too few people perform it because it requires descent to the ground, which is unnatural and rather difficult, especially in the third age. I recommend varying these exercises with a variant known as "super slow" - very slow movement of a weight or slow pushups. This variant leads to recruitment of more muscle units and to significant fatigue of the muscle over a short period of time – exactly what we want to achieve to facilitate strengthening of the muscle. Performance of a very slow squat or a very slow push-up is an excellent way of achieving stimulation of muscle for fatigue and aching within one or two repetitions, and significantly shortens the length of the training.

- Each of the exercises presented here should be performed occasionally until muscle failure in an all-out fashion. The initial weight will of course depend on the capability of each trainee, but I recommend starting with a weight bar without any weights, for example. Keep in mind that super-exercise training is for your entire life, so that if we perform weight training all our life, increasing the weight to place a greater load on the muscle and stimulate it to growth must be done very gradually — unless it is important to develop our muscles quickly for some reason. So it is, for example, when we work with the kettlebell weight, we start at 8 kilograms (or 17.6 lb) and then slowly over the years reach 20 kilograms (44 lb) and then 24 kilograms (53 lb). When I perform push-ups, I slowly over the years, increase the difficulty of the exercise and perform it slower or faster, with more repetitions on one hand, with legs lifted, and so forth. In the deadlift exercise we slowly add weight over the years, in accordance with our basic fitness.

- Weight training can be excellent for you, but it has several downsides. First, it is monotonous, rather boring, and repetitive. In order to reach a good level of strength, one must continue his training over many years, train in the gym with the same exercises over and over again. Very few people are attracted to repetitive and monotonous work with weights, and even fewer people continue with such training their entire lives. Still, in a cost-benefit calculation, a good weight-training program is one of the most important and useful exercise programs we can perform, especially in the third age. Daily performance of strength exercises with body weight is, as far as I am concerned, sufficient for those who do not wish to invest considerable time and effort in daily activity, even if it is spread out over the day. Fifty squats or 20-30 pull-ups, when they are performed with as much variety as possible, are sufficient to maintain excellent fitness and strength over the years. Remember my patient performed 100 classic squats every day without any variation whatsoever. This was his only activity. He continued training to the age of 92 and looked excellent; thin, muscular, and strong. In a correct muscle workout we train the entire muscle, including the tendon that connects it to the bone. Working all types of muscle fibers is no simple task. Running and walking, for example, mostly recruit one type of muscle, the slow-twitch muscle fibers, whereas the fast-twitch muscle fibers are activated by rapid and dynamic movement such as squat jumps, kettlebell swings or isometric exercises. I always prefer to perform resistance and strength exercises that recruit all types of muscle fibers. Strength and power exercises immeasurably strengthen our bones as well. Strong muscles mean strong bones, which is an important contributor to good functional aging.

Advanced body weight exercises such as calisthenics are an excellent way for the young and athletic amongst us to develop their body well. Different versions of push-ups, dips, advanced pull-up bar work, handstands, one-legged squats, and utilizing the urban environment – benches, beams, pull-up devices and more – all develop a super-strong body, immeasurably more than working out in a gym with weights with monotonous exercises. The street workout movement, much like parkour, moved physical activity out of sterile blocks and into body-weight work in the urban environment. (Parkour is a method based on French military obstacle-course training in which one uses his body to overcome obstacles, going from one point to another in the fastest and most efficient way possible.) This is a classical street movement, just like the skateboard movement in its inception.

4.2 SPEED

The most critical components for immediate survival are speed and agility. In the past, the speed of communication between senses and muscles is what determined the success of hunting, as well as success in avoiding falling prey to other animals. Are things different today? Not really. Even today, rapid muscle response can save our lives. Even in today's day and age, in our relatively safe and sleepy society, there are situations in which we must rapidly leap aside or backward, to avoid being run over by a car or cyclist. A far more common scenario, which unfortunately occurs more and more often as we age, is the sudden loss of balance due to bumping into some object on the ground, such as a rug or the edge of a sidewalk. If we fail to extend our foot rapidly enough forward, we will, quite literally, fall on our faces. Falling down in the third age may well end in an unpleasant fracture and lead to hospitalization, surgery and other risks, as well as a sharp decrease in functionality and quite often in all-too-avoidable death.

Suffice it to say that speed and agility are an essential condition for success in many sports. The way children move is an excellent example of the physical capabilities the ancient human hunter had to develop. Children's movements are extremely varied, and include leaps, sprints, rolls and all sorts of games. A considerable part of their movement is devoted to rapid motion and sudden changes in direction, such as in the game of catch. Small children do not sedately wander here and there; they usually run.

The sports children favor almost always involve rapid movement – soccer, basketball, athletics, tennis and the like.

Sadly, in Western society, when childhood and adolescence end, rapid and agile movement end as well. From that moment onwards, most of our time is devoted to study, work and building a family. And as the years go by, we become sedate, responsible, thoughtful people. The game of catch disappears almost entirely and is replaced by sitting on our favorite couch or, at best, running or walking slowly, linearly on a treadmill.

Adult activity is almost the exact opposite of childhood activity. While childhood activity is spontaneous, inconstant, frame-free, rapid and agile, "adult" movement is preplanned, set in time and place, slow, and predictable. While children use the playground environment or the yard and play with other children, the adult's movement environment is mostly sterile and devoid of stimuli (other than, perhaps, the voice of their trainer) and interaction.

I strongly recommend preserving the rapid, agile childlike and spontaneous movement component in our daily movement menu. Here are a few examples of exercises that will help implement this recommendation:

- **Rebounding** - this exercise (see detailed instructions in Chapter 3) is one of the best exercises to preserve the rapid and spontaneous movement component, as all of our muscles are rapidly activated in jumping. Any variation of rebounding will automatically include rapid movement as well, for example, the renowned jumping jacks in which the arms are swung and legs are spread during the jump (instructions for this exercise are also detailed in Chapter 3). That is why I recommend you perform several rebounds in place several times a day.

- **Sprinting in place** - this is another excellent exercise and it is recommended you perform it often.

- **Shadowboxing** - fast coordinated movements are the hallmark of martial arts. Very few people have the motivation to pursue this line of training for many years. But why not enjoy some fighting moves? Drop into a half squat, raise your fists and punch the air, just as if you were punching a boxing bag. Lift a stick and wave it around as if it is a sword slicing through the air.

Rapid movement can be added on to almost any hobby or common motion. For example, when you swim, I recommend breaking your swimming routine with a single lap sprint, or by a semi-squat followed by a leap outside the water, or leaping out and then back in, like a dolphin. When you go for a walk, stop for half-a-minute and then run or rebound in place, or even jump rather than run. In the gym, you can swing a light hand weight quickly. You can ride a stationary bicycle quite rapidly.

An excellent hobby which greatly improves the brain function is ping-pong. Here, the rapid movement is interwoven with coordination in a hobby which is safe to practice at any age. Each super-exercise category can be varied by rapid performance. The kettlebell exercises, for example, can be performed deliberately at the fastest possible speed. Pull-ups can be performed explosively. Push-ups can be accompanied by hand clapping. The slow qigong exercises can be practiced with fast movements. Facial exercises can be performed very rapidly, and of course, different accessories such as juggling balls or sticks can be used at a fast pace as well. Advanced athletes can practice jumping explosively from one bar to another (a monkey-like exercise called lache) or learn muscle-ups.

4.3 COORDINATION

The coordination component is the only one involving our entire brain out of all the physical movement components. That is why the incorporation of coordination in our daily movement menu is vital to preserving our brain in a healthy state over the years.

"Standard" physical activity, such as walking, running, swimming or strength exercises, does not require massive brain involvement. These activities are, by nature, monotonous and repetitive, performing the same movement over and over again at the same speed and along a straight pre-determined line. The brain can be put on neutral and you can watch television, listen to music, or speak on the cell phone during a standard activity. In contrast, the brain is optimally activated when it is totally focused on a specific physical activity, for example, when a series of complex actions must be performed in precise and rapid sequence, such as during ballgames, martial arts, or dancing. During these complex activities, our brains are completely engaged in the movement, and our attention is focused 100% within the movement and dedicated to its proper and precise performance. The same applies to activities that involve danger such as skiing or skateboarding, or maneuvers that have no room for error, such as when we walk barefoot outside or on a thin rope or on a beam. Under such circumstances the brain is totally focused on the task to avoid a fall, collision, or injury at any cost. Such engagement keeps our brains in optimal condition and prevents, or at least postpones to some extent, the development of threatening old-age diseases such as dementia or Parkinson's. Activities involving quick movements where a mistake or an error is punished by pain, injury or losing are primarily appropriate for the first decades of our lives. In advanced ages, most people do not actively engage in physical activity involving immediate danger. Nonetheless, we must be vigilant to daily train the ability of the brain to focus completely on complex movement. Below is a list of activities which engage the brain and the body in movement requiring coordination and concentration suitable for the third age and for sedentary individuals.

- **Tai Chi and Qigong** - these ancient Far Eastern movement arts are scientifically proven to prevent Parkinson's. They're also effective in neurological rehabilitation, prevention of falls, and more. In China, it is easy to practice these arts, for in the morning hours there are large groups of people who gather daily to train outdoors. In the West, I recommend finding a teacher, studying at least a few basic movements, and practicing them every day for short durations. Their daily performance is simple and enables training of the brain and preserving its ability to control complex activities requiring concentration.
- **Dance** - folk dancing and ballroom dancing are both excellent ways to train the mind and the body. Beyond the training itself, these dances are also performed in interaction with other people, a fact which very much enriches the physical and mental experience.
- **Music** - it is better to learn to play an instrument at any age, in my opinion, than to learn a new language or solve crossword puzzles. Playing a musical instrument is a sort of a super-exercise because it cultivates our coordination. Music is not easy to learn or simple

to perform, and only few people gravitate towards it. But it is an amazing skill, once you have an instrument at home, enabling you to play as much as you like every day and add a layer of complexity and creativity that tunes and invigorates your brain. There are two musical activities readily available to all of us anytime, anywhere. The first is drumming. We can, for example, drum on our thighs or on our chests or on a table at any given moment as an accompaniment to some music we hear or imagine. The second is singing and humming. The two can be combined, creating a musical interlude in our lives.

- **Walking barefoot** - when we walk barefoot outside, the brain immediately focuses on our movements, because the activity becomes more dangerous as we go along; we might stumble or step on a sharp object. Walking barefoot has been proven to improve memory and concentration by the active engagement of the brain.
- **Rebounding variations** - practice rebounding exercises where the exercise shifts every few repetitions, spontaneously. This will immediately engage your brain.
- **Juggling** - throwing balls in the air and catching them is a very complex movement, but can be learned through repetitive training. It is highly recommended and is very enjoyable.
- A spontaneously performed super-exercise forces the brain to "invent" the nature of the exercises, their order, their intensity, and the number of repetitions. All these, in combination with the recommendation to constantly vary the exercise, will do a fine job in engaging your brain in the movement of the exercise.

4.4 BALANCE

Balance is the response of the brain to data input from three sources; the balance organ (the vestibular portion of the inner ear), the joint sensors that report the location of the joints and muscles, and the eyes. The last component is the only one regularly examined at the doctor's office. Brain injury due to excessive alcohol consumption or various diseases will immediately negatively impact one's balance.

In the third age, each of these data sources undergoes injury and degeneration. The data integration capacity of the brain is also impaired. All this leads to a severe, well-known problem in medicine – third age falls. A fall can be dangerous in every age and all of us fall quite often in life. It is inevitable, especially if we engage in sports such as soccer, basketball, judo, skateboarding or surfing. However, in the third age, due to the degeneration of the bone and the impairment of the instincts, a fall can be lethal. A hip fracture is a terrible blow that should be avoided at all costs. That is why daily balance training is one of the most important movement components in the life cycle.

Below, are a few exercises recommended to help train your balance:

- The jumping exercise - this is a classic balance exercise, especially if it is varied with leaps to the sides, forward and backwards. The legs practice rapid movement and changes in direction, which helps strengthen the stabilizing muscles and daily training of the brain. When we begin leaping on one foot, the brain is immediately awakened and begins working hard to enable us to remain standing. If we close our eyes for a few seconds while jumping , we then further challenge our brain (which must now rely exclusively on the inner ear and joint-muscle sensors, since the seeing component is blocked).
- The "Chinese equilibrium" exercise - this excellent exercise can be made even more challenging by closing your eyes as you perform it.

 The Chinese equilibrium exercise is exercise number 8 in the attached exercise clip

- As you walk, try to follow a straight line on the ground as if you were an acrobat walking on a rope
- Descend to a squat variant that trains balance: stand with heels tightly together, with your feet facing outwards at 45 degrees, and then descend. You will discover that you need to balance yourself on your tiptoes.
- Stand on one leg. In the third age, it is recommended you do so near a chair or table in case you lose your balance and need to grab hold of something to steady yourself.
- Any martial arts-derived movement will train your balance. For example, shifting your weight from foot to foot when your legs are spread while at the same time extending your fist forward.

4.5 FLEXIBILITY

Flexibility is another word to describe the range of motion of each of the joints in our body. Each joint has a maximal range of movement. For example, the functional range of motion of the pelvis and the thigh when we walk is not very wide, but it is certainly sufficient to walk. The maximal range, on the other hand, would be accomplished by lowering one's self to the ground in a split.

Gymnasts, yogis and contortionists are generally individuals who are genetically endowed with a greater range of motion than the rest of us. So, too, are Ehlers-Danlos syndrome patients. This syndrome is a group of genetic disorders deriving from injury to the body's connective tissues that are indicated by chronic pain, hyper flexibility and instability of the joints. Training to extend the range of motion and to stretch tendons and joints is, in my opinion, a total waste of time — and the research supports this. There is no biomechanical significance to being able to touch the ground with your palms without bending your knees. True, this exercise may result in longer and more flexible tendons, but this may actually impair your muscle strength. In contrast, a good movement will generate good flexibility without the need for exercises in which you stretch to the utmost limit of your ability.

We must practice functional flexibility every day. In other words, we need to move all of our joints daily. That is why, once a day, you should move your neck in every possible axis. Perform shoulder exercises and range exercises for your back and feet every day and, if possible, more than once.

It is important to emphasize a good length of the Achilles tendon. Ensure you can drop down to a squat without lifting your heels from the floor in any way. This is a very important biomechanical range. On the other hand, there is no need to practice ballet-style "pointe."

4.6 ENDURANCE

Cardiovascular exercises, aka aerobic exercises, have won positive attention over the past few decades, as the false myth that long-distance running burns calories and helps lose weight has become widespread.

Do the heart or lungs require any training? After all, they work 24 hours a day, regardless of what the rest of the body is doing. Our heart beats around 70 times a minute, 4,200 times an hour, 100,000 times a day. Our lungs are constantly inhaling and exhaling.

What we are actually training in long-distance running and swimming, when a regular pulse and pace are maintained, are not the heart and lungs, but the limbs' muscles. Every muscle system regulates its blood flow locally. And every muscle adapts to a repetitive movement. The heart and the lungs never tire as they are biologically built to work nonstop unlike the rest of our muscles that have a limit of to how much work they can produce. Take, for instance, a cyclist at peak condition who can ride hundreds of miles a day and put him on the basketball court. You will likely discover he is out of breath within a few minutes. His muscles are adapted to long-distance cycling but not to the explosive sprints and jumps of basketball.

Does our modern world require us to possess the capability of performing an absolutely artificial activity, such as running in a straight line for miles and miles over hours? Of course not. Should we travel back in time over 2000 years, we would find that the capacity to run for long distances was never important to our ancestors and was certainly never trained for, with the sole exception of the inclusion of the marathon in the Olympic Games. And how many people ever trained for or participated in those?

Are hours spent on running or walking every week therefore a waste of time? Well, no, because any body movement is good. Running stimulates blood and lymph circulation, results in the release of adrenaline and an ecstatic "runner's high" and strengthens our willpower and perseverance.

As a rule, though, long endurance exercises are not super-exercises, for much time must be set aside for them, preventing them from being performed whenever we desire. Furthermore, they cannot be performed at any age and any health condition. An additional downside of aerobic exercises is that they are monotonous exercises performed on a straight surface – a surefire recipe for accelerated wearing down of joints and periodic visits to the orthopedic surgeon. Those who enjoy running and want to safeguard themselves from injury are invited to continue to do so, but should vary their running and support it with the various super-exercises.

Endurance, in its spiritual dimension, is a very important resource in our daily lives. The ability to withstand pressure and persevere at work, at a relationship or at a given training method has incredible importance in our complex lives. Prolonged aerobic training, particularly if it becomes marathon or triathlon training, brings us to the outer limits of our mental capacity. We must face our inner demons who whisper, "Why are you doing this? Step down. This knee pain is bad. You are hurting yourself." This aspect of training is important and exists not only in running, the triathlon and the tour-de-France, but also in rigorous military training or martial arts – training that brings us to the edge. Quite naturally, most of us feel no special need to bring ourselves to the edge.

A sports magazine might enthusiastically report that ten thousand people ran the Berlin marathon. The more accurate headline would be that 86,620,000 people in Germany (minus 10,000) did **not** run the Berlin marathon. An individual watching the marathon might conclude that many people run the marathon, but the proportion of runners to the general population in minute. That is very good, for a marathon can kill. Not everyone who runs a multi-participant marathon completes the track.

Prolonged-endurance exercises are perceived as "calorie burners." In fact, the body only burns a few calories during those exercises, particularly if one runs at an unchanging and comfortable pace. Prolonged workouts result in greater appetite in the trainees, and the burned off calories will return rapidly in a large meal. Those who wish to prevent excess weight believe that rigorous running exercises will achieve that goal – and they are right. But the price is accelerated wear and tear of the joints and an immediate rise in weight if the individual ceases, for any reason, to train.

Studies have now demonstrated that intensive interval workouts are far more efficient than endless endurance exercises. Fifteen minutes of training, three times a week is sufficient to raise the muscle mass and lead to elimination of fatty tissue even two days after the training. The problem is that such intensive training is suitable for very few people, those who are attracted to intensity and achievements, and they, too, will abandon it at some point given its monotonous and repetitive nature.

Those who so desire can intensify any super-exercise and transform it into an intense interval exercise.

Athletic jumps with squats, all-out sprints in place (bringing your knees to your chest while running in place), animals walks for half-a-minute or calisthenics on a pull-up bar are extremely intense exercises. Since we slowly build up muscle mass over consistent and daily training, training that is performed over the course of an entire day, our metabolic rate will rise and so will our basic calorie burn. It is true that the ability to run long distances is not trained for in super-exercises, but I do not believe we require this ability today. To survive and live long functional lives, the components of strength, speed, coordination, balance and good posture are much more important.

4.7 POSTURE

This is a critically important component. Posture is in fact the balance between the various muscle and bones, fascia and other connective tissue elements like cartilage and sinews. Weakness in one of these components, or absence of symmetry between different elements will result in a distortion of our posture. The distortion might be inconspicuous, such as a slightly outthrust chin, or one slightly drooped shoulder, or it may be easily observable such as a bent back or a flat foot.

A strong aligned, symmetrical body will hold all bones and joints in their proper place throughout one's entire life cycle. That is why the super-exercise model emphasizes constant awareness of erect, symmetrical, and properly-balanced posture. This is one reason why rebounding and bar exercises are such good exercises, for they return us, again and again, to good posture. There are excellent posture and movement exercise systems such as Alexander and Feldenkrais. But as in any system, no one practices these methods daily other than those who teach them and a few dedicated students.

We therefore require very simple exercises that will return us again and again to an integrated and stable posture. The basic qigong exercises answer this need, in particular, the mountain exercise and the shoulder movement exercise (see instructions in Chapter 3).

Tucking in your chin, straightening up, and standing with legs at shoulder width and feet parallel to each other with a loose but slightly tense body (like a resting tiger) are actions that can be, and should be, done dozens of times a day. Don't even call it training or exercise. I recommend first performing some manner of super-exercise (e.g., jumping or qigong exercise), and stop immediately after the exercise, stand with good posture for a single deep breath, and then carry on with your routine. That is how the body can be provided with a stimulus to maintain a good posture throughout the day.

CHAPTER 5

Super-Exercise Training and the Life Cycle

By now you surely understand that the motto of the super-exercise training is "every day, all day, for your entire life, anywhere." When I say "your entire life," my meaning is quite literal – movement that begins at age zero and lasts to our final years, and which not only preserves our abilities over the years, but even improves them over time. The current chapter considers the characteristics of movement in each stage of the life cycle, focusing on the first two decades of life and the latter decades, and presents specific recommendations for super-exercises during these ages.

5.1 THE EARLY YEARS

FIRST YEAR OF LIFE

In their first year of life, infants do not yet walk, and their activity, especially in the early months, is no more than eating, messing their diapers and wailing, with the occasional smile bursting out to get parents to forget everything else. Physical connection with the infant is critical during this year. I would massage my children with oils to stimulate their muscles. There are excellent child massage books and it is a very pleasant way to calm a baby down before putting him to sleep. I also recommend walking as much as possible with the baby in a sling in order to stimulate its senses outside the house. It goes without saying that short sunbaths are a must. There is no need to sterilize every surface the infant comes into contact with or crawls upon; a little dirt can only strengthen and train the baby's immune system.

My family's house is also the home of two old and rather stinky dogs (apologies to Doggy and Thomas) and two furry cats. Every day we sweep out a fur ball the size of a fist. The babies crawl on the floor and in the yard, and in the garden, they crawl on the grass itself. It is important that they grow used to crooked and variable surfaces and to a variety of germs from age zero. Various studies have shown that this will help the child establish a flexible and effective immune system as well as proper motor development.

YEAR ONE TO YEAR SIX

These are the years in which most growth and brain-body wiring occur. This is the first window of opportunity in which parental decisions shape the child's life both physically and emotionally. In these years, children passively absorb the culture they are living in. In a culture where most of us prefer mental to physical work, parents naturally emphasize the development of cognitive learning skills such as the development of language, games meant to stimulate thinking, learning numbers and letters and, of course, staring at screens. This is, in my opinion, a severe error. Effective learning occurs with the entire body and with all senses. The emphasis should therefore be on the development of an optimal neural, muscular, and sensory network through environmental stimuli.

In the United States around half (!) of all children suffer from some chronic illness or another – asthma, obesity, allergies, chronic stomach aches, anxiety, depression, ADHD, disturbed sleep, diabetes, autism, autoimmune diseases (such as celiac), migraines, backaches, recurring ear infections and more. I hope that your child does not suffer from any of the diseases on this grim list, but you surely know at least one child who has been diagnosed with one or more such diseases. How did we arrive at this state? Does it make sense for our children to be quite so sick?

It seems that the challenge facing parents today, that of raising a child who is strong of body and spirit, one who can provide for himself and raise his own family, is greater than ever. Many parents think that all children so young need is love, hugs, and positive reinforcement, with everything else being secondary. So it is not terrible to give a child junk food if that is what he wants; it is all right to let a three-year-old stare at a tablet for two hours, for it develops his brain and that is what he wants to do; it is not terrible to let him go to sleep late; and it is fine to purchase for him colorful toys, because it is fun and that is what he wants.

Love is indeed important, vital even, but it is not sufficient to raise a healthy child. The most important necessity in these ages is to develop the body and senses in accordance with the pattern imprinted in our genes. If you are worried about the child not receiving sufficient time on his smartphone, computer, or television, let me reassure you that your infant will complete the lack throughout his life, plus interest.

The various screens put the child's motor system to sleep. It is clear to all of us that spontaneous play with Legos, where the child sits on the floor and activates all his senses and challenges his precise motor skills, develops the imagination and creativity incomparably more than staring at a screen. Screens are like a sedative to the body. They teach the child, from his early years, to still his body and activate only his sight and hearing to take in programs and games that are completely divorced from his environment. The disconnect they provide from the physical environment is immediate and prolonged. So the child learns, early on, to separate himself from his environment and from his body for much of the day, and often during the night as well. While the reality surrounding him is multidimensional, the screens are two-dimensional.

Research in this field for the outcomes of such behavior is far from encouraging; attention disorders, obesity, social isolation, language development impairment, violence, damage to the imagination and more. Various regulatory institutes recommend limiting screen hours today, and certainly in the first years of life. But many parents fall asleep at their posts and fail to realize the enormous damage screens are causing their children. Although regulatory institutions have taken heed of the physical damage caused to children by prolonged sitting and the overload of hectic data projected from the screens, they fail to take into account another big problem, which is the exposure to artificial electromagnetic frequencies. These frequencies completely disrupt our internal communications system and our biological clock that are dependent on environmental energies – the sunlight and the earth's magnetic field.

The most important thing you can do at this stage of your child's life is avoid interfering with it. Their instincts and animal intuition still work rather well during these years. All the child requires is the right environment, and he will do the rest himself. A good environment is one where the child can discover curved surfaces and stimuli for his senses and challenges for his muscles.

In other words, beaches, lawns, trees, bushes, playgrounds, and, if possible, a large, fenced-in trampoline. For urbanites who lack a yard, I recommend they seek out as natural a surface as they can find.

Indoor play areas are one option, though to me they always seemed much like bacterial petri dishes with bad quality air. Almost any apartment can be fitted with a small trampoline.

I recommend using shoes as little as possible. In this way, the

child's feet will be stimulated and he will also learn to look where he is going.

The straight surfaces we walk on put our nervous system to sleep, especially if we wear shoes. This is not how our feet were designed to move. Our toes were designed to open up like a fan and then clench the surface, like apes. Walking on a non-straight surface creates a slightly different system of pressures on the foot. Imagine that you are walking on the beach – every step slightly changes the angle in which the foot meets the sand. When we walk barefoot, our mind automatically becomes active and begins to constantly scan the ground.

In contrast, when the child is always wearing shoes and walks on straight, safe, surfaces, he does not need to stop and look where he is going, and the information-processing capability associated with walking in a field degenerate. In fact, it is lost to the point that even a tiny topographical variation is enough to cause children to suddenly lose their balance as they run or walk, often entangling their legs, even at ages nine to ten. That is why I advise bringing the child's bare feet in contact with crooked, uneven, surfaces as much as possible. In safe areas, such as rubber floored playgrounds, it is always recommended to take off their shoes. Furthermore, I advise encouraging your children to walk as much as possible, as early as possible, and not accustom them to laziness by using a stroller at the age of three or four. You will be surprised to discover that children, even aged eighteen-months-to-two-years can walk for considerable distances. Children love to play and to move their body during these years, and it is important to give them the space to do so and make an effort not to extinguish this joy by seating them to stare at glowing screens.

When I spend time with my children, I always take them to some sort of activity – the yard, a playground, a park, the pool, the ocean or a bicycle ride. To my delight, I have been able to plan my living environment so that even though it is urban, I have a small yard at home, the park is only twenty meters (about 65 feet) away, and the playground is 300 meters (less than 1/2 of a mile) from home. During our activities, I play with my own games beside the children and, occasionally, I play with them spontaneously. I try not to interfere with the children's game. If you are jumping at home next to the kids and invite them to jump as well, they will join you automatically and begin to jump a little as well.

Since most physically active parents limit their activities to blocks, rather than the home, and certainly not near the children, the personal example component is missed. That is why it is important not merely to be active but be seen being active by your children. In this way, you will give them a clear and direct personal example.

When we are at home, I like to occasionally play with the children doing animal walks, play catch with light medicine balls, lift them to my shoulders and perform squats, lift them to the pull-up bar and hang them from it for several seconds (while sheltering them from a fall), or perform various simple TRX exercises such as forward and backward rolls or swinging on the gripping rings. I'll ask them for example, "How high can you jump?" or have them perform a short sprint in place, or I might run with them rapidly in small steps throughout the house (which is very funny and very tiring). My activity with the children is spontaneous and lasts only a few seconds or minutes before I retire. The activity is never defined by time and is always spontaneous.

Several times a week we jump on the big trampoline, always in various changing compositions of children. The large trampoline looks like a mixed martial arts cage. This is a totally safe surface, provided certain ground rules are observed. The trampoline is a genius engineering solution to the absence of non-straight surfaces in urban life, the trampoline surface changes from step to step and from jump to jump.

The constant change of the angle of the foot and of the surface multiplies the efficiency of the jumping and improves neural wiring. In a relatively short time span, the jumper goes through almost all possible movements, while preserving an erect posture and enjoying all the other advantages of this exercise. In short, this is an excellent space that creates a safe solution for the lack of curved and crooked surfaces.

Those who cannot find a playground, or who lack the time or strength to go outside with their children have no choice but to register the child to some class or another. Bear in mind, however, that your child should not be active in this class as if it were the path to a sports career. After a year of judo at the age of four, most chances are that your child will not proceed onwards to an Olympic career, and that is for the best if you value their health. Athletic and acrobatic classes are the better choice, for they develop fundamental movement patterns and emphasize play over competition.

When winter ends, you can take your child, at any age, to a water environment. A pool, an ocean, a lake – all options are good. Water movement will be imprinted on the child's neural system.

Even though the swimming pool is a classic block , it provides the child with an injury-safe environment and more importantly, with a quiet environment in which he can calm down from the constant hum of the digital information all around him. The child also learns to adapt to cold and changes of temperature. Any other class – soccer, basketball, judo or dancing – is of course performed within a block and obligates the child to a rigid system of rules and artificial movement which is only suited for that specific type of sport. On the other hand, when the child swims, he moves in the water just as his distant ancestors did and adapts his naked body to the changes in nature. The monotonous movement and the regulation of breathing contributes to the stabilization of the nervous system during the critical years in which it develops. Swimming in adulthood and in the third age is a super-exercise in and of itself. Since the activity places negligible load on the joints, it can be continued throughout the life cycle, enabling the swimmer to benefit from the great advantage of this activity – relaxation of the nervous system. Sadly, clean and suitable water environments are not available for most of us.

AGES 6-12

The child usually enters school and slowly enters the adult world between these ages, which means long periods of time every day seated on a chair, and staring at texts and images for most of the day. At these ages, children will work out for two hours or so a week in physical education classes in school, and after school will perhaps play with their friends in an environment dependent on where they live. Our influence as parents begins to wind down to weekend activities and, for those who can afford them, longer yearly vacations.

Nonetheless, at these ages, you can already realize that the work you invested in developing physical elements in their first years will guide your child into some sports class, and love of the outdoors, movement and play. It will also generate an excellent basis for learning, good memory and excellent concentration capability.

Parents to children of these ages are usually older and frequently have more than one child. This means that chances are good that they are a bit tired at the end of the day and on the weekends. When the weekend comes, after an entire week of driving the kids around, problem solving, homework help, quality time, work, relationship maintenance, friends and hobbies, I admit that the last thing I want to do is pack up four kids and go gallivanting off into nature while at the same time keeping them from killing each other or disappearing into thin air. And yet, in spite of the difficulties, I strongly recommend you spend time over the weekends and on vacations with the kids in nature, instead of taking them for urban vacations abroad.

Continue playing with your kids at home as well. By this point, a child should be able to pull himself up on the pull-up bar on his own and easily rebound on the trampoline. If the pull-up bar is accessible, encourage the children to constantly stretch themselves, and at some point, they will do so on their own initiative - and constantly. Occasional body-weight practice on the pull-up bar such as swinging, monkey bars and pull-ups is all the child needs at this point. Children are naturally playful, and you can use the repertoire of super-exercises to engage your children and yourself in short intervals of just a few seconds or minutes of exercise. Children love animal walks, they love juggling balls, and they like jumping around. Such playful activity will gradually build up their neuro-muscular system and prepare them for adult and elderly life.

These are also the classic ages in which it is recommended you register the child for a swimming class. Other recommended classes are athletics and general fitness, in which the children play without any clear goal or plan (which is excellent) and without competition. I do not believe there is any point of developing aerobic fitness in the child at this age. As a rule, I don't push my children to engage in any particular hobby. Soccer, basketball, gymnastics and other such sports are likely to cause injuries and direct the child's body and mind to be locked on a specific skill set instead of enjoying the full spectrum of free movement. The box/block composition takes hold in the child's mind and might cast its long shadow throughout his or her life.

Parents that are physically active will prove to be an inspiration to their children, especially if the kids see the parents being active. In contrast, a worn out and tired parent who is constantly hooked up to his Facebook or email, or stares at his television for hours on end will ingrain passivity in his children. They will then learn to fixate on a screen as their first choice in any spare moment they may have.

Just like adults, children today relax in front of screens. Boredom and stress are diluted in a mashup of entertained information and supposedly disappear. We slouch for hours on the sofa and stuff our brains with the equivalent of junk food. Our brains which are designed to synchronize motor actions on the ground, in the water, and on the trees, our brains which are supposed to regulate a body's activities throughout the day, which must serve us in studies and later on at work as well, undergo complete flattening as we spend long hours each day processing completely unimportant information, while operating only a single tiny muscle in our index fingers.

AGES 12-18

Parental influence is minimal during these ages, since children at this age are dangerous, both physically and financially. They've neared their fully-grown body mass, but their brains at this age are on a hormonal vacation. The physical activity in these ages is dependent on many factors and closely competes with social activity and school, not to mention screens. Some adolescents will begin testing the limits of their bodies in various sports fields.

However, most adolescents do not perform the recommended level of physical activity for their age (an hour a day). On the other hand, children of these ages watch an average of more than five hours of television and other screens, combined, a day!

The result of this endless sitting in front of screens begins to be expressed during these early ages, with the body shaped into the chair mold – the back is slightly bent, the chin is thrust out and the shoulders are drooped. At that age group and even before, breathing shifts from the diaphragm to relying on the chest muscles, which starts to build an unhealthy habit of shallow, less efficient chest breathing.

The role of parents in this age is to encourage boys and girls to walk on foot, ride bicycles (real, pedal-driven bicycles, not electric bikes) and go on outdoor activities. But the most important component remains the personal example at home, on the pull-up bar, games/work with the TRX or other bands and classical exercises (push-ups, squats, kettlebell). In conjunction with this, it is important to encourage the children to take short breaks from sitting in front of screens, and of course to practice several super-exercises. Despite the difficulty in influencing children of these ages, this can be done, and the results may surprise you. The story of Roni, one of my patients, demonstrates this.

Roni, a lovely 14-year-old girl, came to see me with her mother to find out why she was the shortest child in the class and if anything could be done about it. Like most of her peers, Roni entered my room with cell phone in hand and her device constantly vibrated throughout the appointment. As we spoke, she admitted she spent around five hours a day staring at her cellular phone, dealing with thousands of WhatsApp messages. Like most teenagers, she performed almost no physical activity (other than sport classes at school), and like other children her age, she suffered from attention disorders and had been on Ritalin for about three years. I will note that I am by no means categorically opposed to Ritalin prescriptions – when they are actually needed. In many cases, there are other, safer alternatives. Physical activity has been proven to significantly improve attention disorders. But how can you convince a girl for whom physical activity is simply not part of her world, to begin to move?

To mobilize Roni to help herself we agreed on a work plan. I explained to her that hanging on a bar at least three times a day for several seconds could extend her body by 1-2 centimeters (½ inch) during the hang, while creating a tight waist and strengthening her hands. And all this in only around a minute of activity a day. Bingo! I got her attention. In addition to the hanging, I recommended to her to purchase a small trampoline and hop on it for twenty seconds, no more than that, three times a day. Roni eagerly adopted the plan.

Two months later I called the parents and asked how the plan was going. It turned out that Roni, to her parents' vast surprise, had decided to register for a dance class twice a week after only two weeks of training. She continued with the exercises I had given her and even increased the duration of rebounding and stretching exercises. She also cut down on her Ritalin, taking it only before tests at school.

So what happened here? Roni, like many of her peers, was completely disconnected from her body. Her life revolved around schoolwork, friends and screens.

If I had recommended to her to sign up to a gym or asked her to be more active, then the project would likely have been doomed to failure, her motivation for change would have remained minimal, and her gym would have remained orphaned. Even if she had persisted in her dance class twice a week, she still would have had five whole days a week of sitting for 15-16 hours in front of a screen. That is why I prepared for her a super easy and super short activity. What's the big deal about jumping a bit and stretching a bit on a pull-up bar? That very same day, the girl began practicing. Since she was young, she was able to immediately reconnect with her body's need to move, and her mind's need to deal with the synchronization of the movement. The result was the dance class that seemingly popped out of nowhere and which is now of great interest to her. The rebounding helped her concentration, and so she has less need of Ritalin. The match was lit and it kindled into a small flame.

5.2 AGES 18-65

The four central decades of our life make up our personal autobiography. Where were we born? To whom were we born? What did we study? What did we work in? With whom were we in social contact? How many children did we have? Our personality is stabilized and grounded during these years, and we gather experiences, shape our beliefs, express our opinions and select our goals. It is in this period of life that most of us first encounter the stress associated with modern life, physical stress deriving from prolonged sitting in front of the computer every day, and mental stress due to insufficient sleeping hours, worries, lack of satisfaction and more. Money also enters the picture at this point, and directly and significantly impacts our lifestyle, the choices we make, and our mental condition.

Simultaneously, time limits begin to play a significant role in our life. How can we best divide our time between work, family, friends, leisure, vacations, and screens, and also find the time to move our body?

In these years, the pattern of our physical movement is grounded. How will our posture look like? How will we move? Where will we move? Most of us understand theoretically that we should nurture our movement or "stay in shape" as it is called, but in practice, every individual develops a unique pattern of movement – a pattern influenced by many factors. These include both internal factors such as mood, energy levels, health, goals, passions, experience, genetics, nutrition, sleep and more, and external factors such as the weather, one's workplace and residence, social and economic status, availability of training facilities and so forth. Some people do no more than the bare minimum; maybe they walk from home to their car and from their car to the office and vice versa. Others cling to hobbies such as cycling, karate, swimming or yoga, and persist in them for many years, even transforming their hobby into a profession. However, most people bounce back and forth between active and non-active phases.

Today, more than any period in human history, we face almost infinite options of how to move our body – be it walking, running, cycling and swimming or tennis, ping-pong, volleyball, CrossFit, TRX, gym classes, weightlifting, and surfing or different types of dancing, yoga, tai chi of various kinds and more. Most people get lost in all these options and either do nothing or occasionally do something that looks to them like physical activity. The absolute majority do not know what correct physical activity is. Quite rightly. Not a single animal in nature needs guidance to understand what good, wise or correct physical activity is. Tigers, dolphins, and coyotes do not require any particular program or system to keep fit or nurture their fitness. All of these animals manage to maintain fantastic fitness and preserve their weight without any classes, devices, trainers or television programs in which fit and sculpted people move from side-to-side-while flinging their limbs every which way, teaching the viewers how to keep in shape. In this chaos of endless possibilities, the super-exercise training model presents clear and simple principles of movement that can be immediately implemented anywhere, at any age and in any health condition. The purpose of the training is clear – preserving and nurturing all our physical capabilities throughout our life cycle. Super-exercises have the power to rescue us from the natural decline of our capabilities. Take Eli, for example, a 60-year-old who visited me due to his elbow pain. Eli is an amateur tennis player who competes in national seniors' tournaments and plays three times a week. He looks great and seems as healthy as an ox. Aside from a slight elbow injury, he is an inspiring example for his peers. Eli loves playing tennis, and his goal is to continue playing as much as he can.

This is an excellent but partial goal and focusing on it exclusively misses the bigger picture. Someday, Eli will not play as well as he does today. It is very rare to see active tennis players prancing around the court at age 80 or 90. At some point, the body can no longer generate the ability required for sprinting and rapid changes in direction. The ability needed for tennis will decline from decade to decade, until it will completely fade away, leaving behind an aching body and completely worn-out joints.

I explained to Eli that he had better start performing exercises right now before he entered a narrowing funnel of capabilities. Hanging on a pull-up bar and light rebounding in place can be easily performed even at advanced ages, but it is recommended that you start training at an early stage, so that you may enter the later decades with a well-trained and energetic body.

I briefly explained to him the importance of the connective tissue to movement and body health, and how one can nurture this element each day. The easiest way to reach a state where movement is spontaneous, light and not burdensome is through daily practice which becomes habitual. Then, just like animals, there is no need to plan or consider the activity. It occurs spontaneously throughout the day, every day of your life. That is why, in these years, I recommend basing movement on a series of super-exercises designed to keep you in shape.

A combination of several exercises in your daily activities will keep you in basic physical fitness and will constitute a comfortable springboard from which to occasionally shift gears and vary or increase your exercises. Even people who are committed to a given hobby or system can spice up their regular exercise with super-exercises that will enrichen their physical repertoire. Super-exercises are an excellent filler for those periods of life in which physical activity declines for various reasons – lack of time, injury, low energy and so forth. Daily practice will preserve all our movement components. This includes daily rebounding, daily hanging on a pull-up bar, squats, breathing exercises, qigong exercises, push-ups and fascia tissue exercises. These will take up no more than several minutes each day, minutes composed of short intervals scattered throughout the day, anywhere you might be. These exercises will train your strength, speed, balance, coordination, breathing, flexibility and posture, and ensure your connective tissue "stays in business" for years. Regardless of what super-exercise you choose, the connection between the body and the mind will be nurtured and safeguarded. I re-emphasize the importance of a daily exercise, and insofar as possible, exercising throughout the day, which means several short exercises a day. Too many people experience a considerable decline in their fitness from the age of 40 onwards. Proper movement and maintaining a strong and wise body are the best way to maintain both good mental and optimal physical health. It is important that we utilize these decades to prepare ourselves well for the final years of our life.

5.3 FINAL DECADES AND THE THIRD AGE: 65-90

The final 20 years of our life are often characterized by complex health situations. Even individuals who are completely healthy coming into the third age accumulate various injuries and surgeries. In the third age we visit the doctor more and more often, and our list of chronic medications begins to lengthen. The body undergoes wear and tear over the decades. And yet, the movement of the body and the connection to the elements of life remains as important and significant as in any age.

There is, however, some good news as well. Time is readily available in our later years, and the cumulative research in this topic unambiguously indicates that there is no upper age limit for fitness development. We have the potential for improvement and change at any age, even if it is minimal. In the third age, safety must come first for we wish to avoid dangerous falls, harm to our joints and muscle strains that may result in a torn tendon. That is why all exercises must be performed with low intensity (except for isometric exercises).

In SET we deliberately choose exercises that counteract specific aging processes. Below is a list of potential ailments and the exercise that best offsets them:

— Muscle loss: isometric exercises, squats, kettlebell/medicine ball
— Loss of connective tissue suppleness: rebounding, qigong exercises, foam roller massages, pull-up bar stretches
— Loss of breathing capacity: breathing and qigong exercises
— Loss of height and erect posture: hanging from a pull up bar, rebounding
— Osteoporosis: rebounding, animal exercises, squats
— Loss of balance and coordination: rebounding variations, kettlebell, spontaneous movement and dancing

REBOUNDING

In the third age it is recommended you start off with 20-40 medical rebounds or light jumps on a trampoline, without completely disconnecting your foot from the surface, and while holding on to a safety rail. After a few weeks or months, one can slowly increase the intensity of the exercise by adding repetitions and slightly higher jumps. The exertion scale should be extremely slow and spontaneous, in order to allow the body to adapt to the movement and properly develop the required muscles and coordination. Once you feel safe enough, you can vary the exercise by flinging your arms to the side, do medical rebounds on a single leg, jumping with legs slightly spread, and various other light versions of the exercise. You will realize how your body slowly, as if of itself, strengthens, and its tonus tightens up. You will spontaneously begin to perform slightly higher rebounding, until you reach even a light athletic jump, where the knees are slightly bent, the arms are flung backwards, and you jump up stretching your hands to the sky. The jumps immediately generate a certain rhythm during the day (or "groove" in the language of dance), as well as more rapid, vigorous movement. One can jump for more and more intervals throughout the day. It is recommended you start and finish the day with a short jumping session.

ISOMETRIC EXERCISES

These exercises are safe to perform at any age. In the third age there are no known side effects, but it is recommended for people with irregular heart rate and/or people on extensive medications or very high and unbalanced blood pressure to perform the exercises carefully and at low and short intensity in the initial weeks and months. For beginners, it is preferable and better to exercise for a very brief interval, no more than three-to-four seconds. The body will strengthen over the years and you will naturally exercise more pressure and recruit more of your muscles, and even reach an all-out level. People who are in frail condition should begin with simple exercises that do not operate many muscle groups. For example, you can crush a tennis ball or another soft ball, or carefully try to lift a chair. Over time, you can also slowly raise the intensity of the exercise.

CLASSICAL EXERCISES

The third age and retiree status are uniquely suited for regular visits to the gym. There are no age restrictions and under proper supervision one can focus on efficient strength exercises, even only once a week.

HANGING

Hanging is an excellent exercise for any age. Beginners in the third age can immediately try to hang, while strictly maintaining the safety of the pull-up bar. People of any age with injuries or shoulder surgeries should perform this exercise extremely carefully and listen attentively to their body. In any event, practice solely hanging for several months for your arm muscles to strengthen, and then begin to slightly vary the exercise.

QIGONG EXERCISES

These exercises are particularly well suited for the third age, and millions of adult Chinese perform them daily. They are slow, easy to perform and completely safe exercises. It is recommended you perform the entire series of exercises as it appears in Chapter 3 and in various YouTube clips every day. It is recommended that you perform the mountain exercise at the beginning and end of the day. You can insert one or more exercise in a sort of endless loop of intervals throughout the day.

KETTLEBELL AND MEDICINE BALLS

These exercises are also excellent for the third age. When I was a child, senior citizens on the beach were training with huge, brown medicine balls. It is, of course, recommended to start off with a lightweight ball or kettlebell of 4-6 kilos (or about 9-13 lb) and raise the weight by a kilo (2.2 lb) or two every few months.

An excellent example for the advantage of the super-exercise training in the third age is the story of my patient, Tova. Tova, 72, reached my clinic for counseling after she'd met with the neurologist treating her for the mild CVA (cerebrovascular attack) she'd suffered. Alongside various medical recommendations that the neurologist had recommended to her, he also told her to walk 5-6 times a week, 40 minutes in each session. "Well, and do you walk?" I asked her. She stared at me sadly. "Not really," she replied. "Only once in a while do I have enough strength to go outside and walk a little".

Tova had never been active physically. So what are the odds that now, at the age of 72, after a CVA and with a long list of medications, she would suddenly take up walking five or six times a week?

"I have a proposal for you," I told her. Within ten minutes, I explained to her about rebounding, showed her how to do it, and we then rebounded together. Her prescription included 20 rebounds in place, over the course of 10 seconds, 3 times a day. That was it. No other super-exercise. As is my custom, I called her a week later to remind her to perform the rebounds (she remembered), and again a week after that. In the phone conversation which took place a month after we met, Tova told me that she was already rebounding 5-6 times a day, and sometimes even 30-40 times. I recommended her to begin to vary her jumps, but not to increase their number. She decided to learn a few isometric exercises from YouTube clips. In our next meeting, three months later, her mood was much improved. She had begun walking two-to-three times a week for 20-30 minutes. I explained to her how she could also vary the monotonous walking.

The super-exercise model constitutes, for me, a tool which enables me to immediately explain the principles of physical movement and recruit the patient during our first meeting. This is a classical win-win situation, which is very rare in medicine The patient gains from immediate initiation of physical activity without committing to long, monotonous and boring activity, and requires no special motivation to get started and I also benefit as I rebound a bit during work.

SET principles can be implemented in the third age even without dedicated exercises. One can easily engage the body and mind simply by inducing variety and novelty. Some examples:

— Sitting on the floor while playing with grandchildren, chasing them around or lifting them and dancing with them
— Doing facial and breathing exercises while walking
— Lifting a shopping bag or a heavy bottle several times
— Lightly dancing and singing while listening to a song
— Spontaneously moving in a swimming pool

CHAPTER 6

Applying Super-Exercise Training in the Clinic

As I explained in Chapter 2, the super-exercise training model was designed to support and cultivate physical activity not only throughout our entire life cycle, but also when suffering from various illnesses. The current chapter focuses on various illnesses and presents recommendations for super-exercises and additional activities that can help improve health. Super-exercise training can be used by therapists of every medical specialty in their clinics. It enables them to provide their patients with clear, simple and easy-to-perform instructions within just a few minutes, and motivate them into immediate action by demonstrating a short exercise in the clinic like rebounding, bar hanging, isometric exercises, or any other exercise appropriately selected from the super-exercise menu. Thus, the patient can be shown how to immediately begin to exercise, imprinting the mantra "every day, all day, everywhere, for your entire life." In my clinic, there is a pull-up bar at the entrance and a kettlebell in the room. When I exercise together with my patient, we both get to work our muscles a bit. From my experience over the years, the chances that a patient will persevere with this type of "formula" of physical activity and implement it, is very high indeed. The super-exercise training is a therapeutic tool, with which we as therapists can force ourselves out of the fixation where we recommend (if at all) the performance of physical activity in classical blocks, a recommendation which is unfortunately rarely implemented by the patient.

Doctors and therapists often prescribe physical activity to their patients. But patients often do not follow. Patients are usually unmotivated and preoccupied with their illness. They find it extremely difficult adhering to 150-300 minutes a week for the rest of their life; walking, running, strength training, as suggested by many medical guidelines. SET, in my experience, is easier to comply with, since by its nature it is short, simple, easy, and can be performed anywhere. Often, beginning slow and low creates a comfortable starting point from which one can successfully advance.

The following recommendations are based on my daily clinical experience instructing and successfully guiding hundreds of patients over the past seven years.

6.1 ORTHOPEDIC PROBLEMS

Rare are the people who will not be forced to undergo some manner of orthopedic rehabilitation at some point during their life. Those who work at a desk job or do no physical activity experience prolonged sitting that destroys the biomechanics of the human skeleton and exposes them to endless problems and pains throughout the skeleton. Those who perform physical activity will at some point suffer from injuries.

The clinical approach to pain deriving from our connective tissue (bones, tendons, cartilage, muscles, fascia) mostly refer only to the specific area of the pain. It is important to understand that orthopedic pain in one part of the body can be caused by orthopedic problems in another part of the body. And in any event, pain influences the entire movement of the body. Furthermore, pain can also be caused or amplified from other routines in our life, such as nutritional patterns, sleep habits, emotional state, medications, and type of work.

Another much neglected part of our body associated with pain is the brain. Faulty neural patterns in the brain will influence the movement and tonus of the muscles.

That is why real recognition of orthopedic pain takes into account not only the diagnosis of the pain area, but also the general condition of the patient. For complete healing to occur, we must look at the totality of the clinical situation. A holistic approach to musculoskeletal problems is rarely found nowadays.

Orthopedic pain, unless it is caused by acute injury, always appears on the background of previous faults in the connective tissue. When we recover from pain, it is always important to repair basic lacks in the body, even if they do not seem to be related to the pain region.

Below are the most common connective tissue impairments:

• **Harm to the function and health of the fascia**

Chapter 7 details how the health of our connective tissue is an essential condition for an orthopedic pain-free life. Our fascia tissue loses its elasticity and smooth movement over the years. A weak, sclerotic, and dried-up fascia tissue impairs our flexibility and strength and as a result we are destined for injury, irritating movement limitations, or chronic pain. Our fascia seems to store emotional stress and trauma over our entire lives, which influences our entire movement and constitutes fertile ground for pain and discomfort.

• **Shortening of certain muscles and lengthening of their opposing muscles**

This is very typical of those who daily sit for many hours, resulting in imbalanced leg muscles. This problem leads to pain, and movement limitations. Such imbalance severely impairs our posture over the years. We become bent, our shoulders droop forward, our core region weakens, the Achilles tendon shortens, and so on.

- **Joint imbalance**

We have already reviewed how, from an early age, we are forced into movement blocks that constrain us to sterile, monotonous, and linear movement. Such movement atrophies our stabilizing muscles that are only activated when the ground is crooked and challenging (for example, by walking barefoot on the beach). A man who walks on a beam, or a stretch rope, mostly uses stabilizing muscles at the sides of his body to move. Slow and weak stabilizing muscles, along with a brain who has forgotten how to use those muscles, are a definite recipe for herniated discs and knee and ankle injuries. These are super-common injuries for people in their forties and onwards who return to a sport that requires strong stabilizers such as basketball, soccer, and skiing after years of sitting and blocked movement.

- **Joint wear and tear**

Just like a car, the body undergoes accumulated wear and tear over the years. The blood supply to the joints declines, the number of stem cells available for the manufacture of new cartilage cells decreases, the bones and tendons accumulate "road dust" in the form of calcification This is the natural process of body aging.

- **Fixation of bad movement and posture frameworks**

This is one of the most important problems which often slips under therapists' radar. How do we move our body throughout our daily life? This is a question which is often left unasked in the clinic. Each of us has a unique body imprint, just like our fingerprints. The body imprint is expressed in the special structure of our skeleton, the sum of the activities we have performed over the years, our injuries, the way in which our body performs operational activities, and the quality of our fascia.

A good, solid treatment or rehabilitation will take into account the correction of bad movement habits and the repair of posture.

Holistic, multisystem appraisal of orthopedic pain is important in any rehabilitative process or orthopedic chronic pain, for it directs us to perform additional therapeutic changes in our lives, rather than just apply a bandage to the current problem.

High quality sleep, inclusion of vital fats such as omega-3 in our nutrition, using herbs such as turmeric and ginger, smoking prevention, taking vitamin C and collagen, stress management, treatment of depression, guided imagery, hypnosis and adaptation of the work environment – all have been scientifically proven to prevent arthritis and orthopedic pain. That is why it is recommended you add them to your training or physical therapy.

Our connective tissues are extremely influenced by our lifestyle and nutritional choices, the nature of our activities, our time management, and our mental and social status.

A chronic health condition also serves as fertile ground for the development of skeletal pain symptoms. For example, if you are diabetic, the odds are that at some point you will begin to suffer from injury to your tiny blood vessels. The significance of such an injury is that your muscles and tendons will be supplied with less blood. And if you don't move at all, that means that your lymphatic system will also not drain the muscles properly. The road ahead is then open for a variety of orthopedic problems in every area of the skeleton.

Regardless of the area suffering from injury, we must always consider the entire picture, and carefully examine what weak points our lifestyle contains. We must also take into account metabolic and physiological vulnerabilities, even if they seemingly have no connection to the aching knee. Furthermore, it is well known today that our connective tissues are strongly influenced by electric currents. Robert Becker, a well-known American orthopedic surgeon, performed a series of experiments in which he demonstrated that the bone is, in fact, a semiconductor which can transform physical stress into electrical currents. (His book "The Body Electric" is illuminating, no pun intended.). The brain is an electric, electromagnetic organ. Our environment is electromagnetic – the sun and the planet charge us up in various ways with electrons and electric currents.

When we are maladapted to our environment — when we sit in a neon-lit office with glaring blue screens surrounding us all day and a not inconsiderable portion of the night, disconnected from direct contact with the earth and feeding on a diet low in vital components — the result will be a weak and dehydrated connective tissue. That is why we are seeing so many orthopedic problems at such a young age, and why osteoporosis is a global affliction. That is why we suffer from so many injuries even though we barely move. And that is why most of us hit our third age with physical functionality near zero, and with agonizing skeletal aches.

As orthopedic problems are always expressed in pain, I do not know anyone suffering from them who has not tried anti-inflammatory and anti-pain medication at some point. When the pills and physiotherapy are not enough, doctors move on to more invasive procedures, including injections, steroids, medical marijuana and more. When these treatments fail, quite a few people arrive at surgical treatments, such as arthroscopy, spinal surgery, shoulder surgery, foot surgery and more. No one wants to find themselves on this track. So what can be done?

Given the difficulty of finding an orthopedic surgeon or physio-therapist with a holistic, integrative perspective, I recommend you do the detective work yourself, try to identify what kind of health imbalance you are suffering from - and then correct it.

6.11 LOWER BACK PAIN

Lower back pain is in fact a variety of clinical symptoms which all of us experience or will experience at some point. These pains are the legacy of our evolutionary journey to walking upright on two legs, to our modern chairbound life, and the old, calcified age most people reach today – but most of all, to the absence of physical activity. Nonetheless, in many cases, back pain is triggered by high-level stress or depression and anxiety. There are also rarer conditions in which chronic back pain indicates an inflammatory skeletal disease (such as arthritis or ankylosing spondylitis) *or a cancer spreading metastatic secondary growths to the skeleton.* Another common risk factor is smoking. Studies have shown that smokers tend to develop more chronic back pain than non-smokers, and that people with chronic back pain who quit smoking report less pain than those who persist.

That is why it is important to treat these problems seriously, and try to solve the underlying problem, and not just focus on the back pain itself.

In the acute pain stage, whether it is strained or torn fascia, disk rupture, muscle cramp, or sciatic nerve inflammation (the longest nerve in the body which starts in the spinal cord and passes through the buttocks, hips and back of the leg), it is recommended you reduce the biomechanical load from the back and cool down not only the painful area, but the entire body, with cold baths or showers. Since sudden exposure to cold water might be difficult for some, I suggest adapting to cold showers or baths as a preventative measure (more on cold exposure in Chapter 9).

I usually recommend lying on your back on a mattress, with your ankles resting on a chair, and lightly rock your back from side to side. It is best you avoid prolonged sitting as much as possible.

Furthermore, I recommend exposing yourself as much as possible to the sun (for vitamin D which has anti-inflammatory properties), and consume plenty of anti-inflammatory foods, such as turmeric, omega-3, ginger, cruciferous vegetables, and more.

One can, of course, also take anti-pain pills. However, the problem with these medications, beyond their immediate side effects, is that they mask the pain enough for the individual to continue with the destructive behaviors that have generated the pain. They then maintain those activities or behaviors, thereby worsening the situation.

There are several local mechanisms that can drive lower back pain, including spinal vertebrae instability, shrinkage, inflammation and dryness of fascia tissue, or a severely slipped disk that applies pressure on a nerve. These mechanisms are usually enabled due to faulty movement and posture, coupled with other possible complications (such as stress, depression, smoking, faulty nutrition, various diseases and more).

Strangely enough, there is no consensus in the medical world on what causes backaches. So be careful and wary of a diagnosis such as "inflammation" or "spasm of muscle" or "slipped disk" or "bad posture" as these terms are generalities. Lack of a true understanding of the causes of backaches all too often leads to treatment modalities that are no better than placebos.

In the initial days and weeks of pain, it is recommended you avoid whatever is causing it, such as prolonged standing or sitting, or a specific yoga exercise.

The exercises I recommend for back pain are suitable to perform regardless of the specific mechanism of the pain. Based on the diagnosis of the mechanism and of basic movement impairments usually performed by a professional, it is possible to prepare a correct and precise action plan later on, in order to prevent future pain and enable free movement. I very much recommend continuing to move by performing exercises that will not activate or stimulate the back.

Below are a number of exercises that will help ameliorate the pain:

- **Hanging on a pull-up bar** - From the very onset of backache , one can begin with hanging on a pull-up bar (see Chapter 3), everyone in accordance with his strength and level, up to 30 times a day if possible. This exercise is excellent for most people. However, if you are feeling uncomfortable or too tense, or if this exercise is painful for you, you should avoid performing it. Hanging on a pull-up bar immediately reduces the pressure on the lower back and gently stretches out the connective tissue. While hanging, you can perform one or two box breaths, further relaxing yourself.

- **The mountain exercise** - You can also, from the very beginning, perform the mountain exercise (see Chapter 3) with your stomach muscles contracted. This exercise will move your pelvis and legs in a light squat, and your hands and shoulders in circle-like motions. Since your back remains stationary, it will not hurt. Repeat the exercise several times slowly, breathing deeply, to soothe the body and cause your brain to work symmetrically on both sides of the body, utilizing gentle coordination. In my experience, the work on the brain is just as important as the work on the painful organ or anatomic area.

- **Shoulder movement exercise** - This exercise (see Chapter 3) is excellent for the acute pain stage. Perform this gentle wave motion throughout the day.

- **Light stretches of the back** - Those who are capable of painlessly descending to squat sitting definitely should do this exercise several times a day, for crouching in this position immediately relieves the load on the lower back.

- **The big three of Dr. Stuart McGill** - These are three exercises to stabilize the spinal muscles taken from "Train Core the Right Way" by Dr. McGill.
- **Gentle fascia exercises with a rubber ball for the palms and feet** - Seemingly, these areas have nothing to do with the lower back, but massages can help the entire body. In Korean acupuncture and reflexology, you use the palms and the feet to influence the entire body.

Even in a condition of acute back pain, you can exercise other parts of the body, as long as you are careful to keep the back straight and the abdominal muscles contracted. Isometric exercises (see Chapter 3 for examples) can be done; like trying to lift a chair weight work with the upper body; or even gentle swimming with flippers or free movement in the water are all examples of exercise that can be done even while in acute pain. You can also, of course, perform facial exercises and the "gorilla" exercise.

Seemingly, none of these exercises have anything to do with the area of pain. However, I believe that focusing exclusively on the painful organ is wrong. When one part of the body is suffering, then the entire body suffers. That is why I always recommend the performance of general exercises that are not connected directly to the problematic region. Light physical activity during the acute-pain phase improves the blood and lymphatic fluid circulation in the body and improves one's mood, which can often be depressed during the acute pain phase.

PREVENTION OF BACK PAIN

Prevention is always the best therapy. As Benjamin Franklin once said, "An ounce of prevention is worth a pound of cure." A meticulously performed daily dose of exercises that address proper posture, strengthen the back muscles, strengthen the posterior chain, promote diverse movements, and broaden the movement range of each of the joints is the best way to avoid orthopedic problems.

Below are a few dedicated back pain prevention exercises:

- Fascia exercises are a must to preserve a healthy back. Rebounding, stretching and foam rolling should be integrated into our daily routine.
- Deadlift - the deadlift is the number one exercise to strengthen the lower back. Although it is a very simple exercise, it is not a readily available option for most of the population.
- Squat - this is the next most efficient exercise after the deadlift, particularly a squat with weights (see Chapter 3).
- Hanging on a bar - the hanging exercise (see Chapter 3) makes the body more symmetrical and "irons out" any asymmetry we may have accumulated throughout our lives, if only for the duration of the exercise. During the hanging exercise, the body receives and delivers a uniform and symmetrical message to the brain.
- Animal walks - these simple exercises (see Chapter 3) strengthen our back without placing any load on it whatsoever (unless we are carrying one of our children).
- Isometric exercises - these exercises (see Chapter 3) are a more readily available alternative to the deadlift. Various chair exercises are excellent. The towel exercise imitates the deadlift and works on most of the body's muscles. It is recommended to perform each of

these exercises with abdominal muscles consciously contracted as this will also automatically contract the back muscles at the height of the abdomen. This contraction creates muscle tension that stabilizes the lower back vertebrae and prevents sharp movements that might result in injury.

6.12 SHOULDER PAIN

The shoulder is a wonderfully complex organ designed to enable movement in any possible direction. The hand, which begins at the shoulder, is a wonder of evolutionary creation and enables us to perform all the subtle movements that humanity developed throughout history including, for example, the construction of complex tools, writing and the arts. Unfortunately, the modern shoulder is a rather miserable joint, for monotonous sitting unbalances the shoulder muscles, leading to a collapse of the shoulder downwards and forwards. What increases the misery of the joint even more is the fact that it is subject to calcification and various tendon tears. It is also associated with our shoulder blades, which are cramped, misaligned and weak in most people. Shoulder problems and injuries are extremely common and have been dubbed with scary titles such as "frozen shoulder," "impingement syndrome" and "rotator cuff tear."

What exercises should you perform during acute shoulder pain? I recommend the following symmetrical all-body exercises that involve the shoulder joints, and suggest that you continue to train your body persistently, and as many times a day as possible:

- Shoulder rotation exercise - this exercise moves the shoulder blade, but not the shoulder joint, and it is therefore excellent and heals many patients. The exercise delivers a message to the brain that the body is in a symmetrical state, balanced, stable and moves very well. In addition, it circulates the blood and the lymph in the shoulder area.

- Hand dancing exercises - these (see Chapter 3) are gentle and easy to perform exercises even during acute pain, and they are good for further pain prevention as well. The shoulder is gently mobilized through several different planes with this exercise. This is a crucial in preventing the dreaded shoulder freeze.

- Rebounding - rebounds (see Chapter 3) are also an excellent exercise in which the shoulder is shaken up and down rapidly. That is why I recommend increasing the number of daily rebounds during shoulder injury.

- Isometric exercises - these exercises (see Chapter 3) are a good way to activate every joint without even moving them. That is why they, too, constitute part of the recommended menu in any orthopedic situation.

- Hanging exercises - partial tears and stress of the biceps tendons are quite common problems. Hanging bar exercises (see Chapter 3) immediately place the shoulder in a neutral and balanced position, and in most cases are completely safe to perform. It is especially excellent in cases of inflammation and problems in the anterior shoulder tendons. Nonetheless, in case of a sprain or an unstable shoulder, or immediately after shoulder operations, it is recommended to avoid the hanging bar exercise. If you do still perform it, do so with maximal caution.

Is it recommended to move the shoulder even when it is painful? Or is it better to listen to the pain and move the shoulder only to the point that it starts hurting? This is an excellent question.

For simple sprains of shoulder tendons, one can certainly charge into the pain with a powerful massage or a stretching exercise your physiotherapist can give you and explain how to perform. In cases of tears and calcifications, the picture is more complex, and my recommendation to people who are not attuned to their body is to consult with a physiotherapist specializing in shoulder problems.

In cases where the shoulder problems become chronic, it is recommended, with professional consultation, to maintain the ranges of movement, even if the movement is accompanied by pain.

PREVENTION OF PROBLEMS IN THE SHOULDER JOINT

The exercises recommended for acute conditions are, of course, excellent for further pain prevention and good maintenance of the shoulders. In addition, the shoulder is very fond of strength and power exercises. That is why all the kettlebell exercises and all the pull-up bar exercises are superb movements to develop a well-balanced and comprehensive system for the entire shoulder. It is important to move the shoulder throughout its range every day to circulate the blood around it and prevent excessive depositing of calcium.

6.2 DIABETES

The appearance of widespread diabetes over the past century is far from accidental. Diabetes is a classical disease of environmental maladaptation. Stick a man in the office, hook him up to a computer, cell phone, tablet and printer, let him eat junk food, allow him to vegetate in front of the television, and you will get a train wreck in the making - a diabetes train wreck. Medical research indicates that sugar is far from the only factor that can push our metabolism in the direction of diabetes; almost any environmental change leading to environmental maladaptation can do the same. Lack of vitamin D, environmental toxins, absence of physical activity, smoking, artificial sweeteners, imbalance between the friendly bacterial flora in the intestine and the pathogenic bacteria, nutritional lacks, gluten consumption, electromagnetic radiation and additional factors significantly raise the risks of diabetes. The pharmaceutical way of treating diabetes helps to delay the appearances of the disease complications in some cases, but does not address the primary factors.

My recommendation to diabetic patients is to carefully examine the imbalances in their life and to try to change them. Physical activity has been proven in many studies to improve the sugar levels in the blood just as well, and perhaps even better than, medications. For example, a review of research performed by the American Heart Association (AHA) and published in the official guidelines of the association in 2008 found that physical activity reduces the levels of HbA1c (glycated hemoglobin) by 0.8%, on the average, an improvement similar to that of medications.

Physical activity improves insulin sensitivity and supports a better metabolism of fats, playing an important role in weight management. It was found that meticulously observing regular physical activity reduced diabetes patients' risk of suffering from strokes and heart diseases. It is therefore extremely important for diabetes patients to engage in physical activity.

What physical activity is recommended for diabetes patients?

- Muscle development and strengthening - the most beneficial activity for diabetic patients is to develop and strengthen their muscles. A good and proper muscle mass results in reduction of the blood sugar levels. That is why I recommend you make use of a fitness trainer and train for at least several months in a gym, in order to study the exercises and understand how to develop muscles. In conjunction with that, I recommend daily work with a kettlebell (see Chapter 3) and isometric exercises (see Chapter 3) to rapidly engage and develop your muscles.

- Rebounding - one of the most severe problems of diabetics is small vessel disease. The heart, the retina of the eye and peripheral nerves therefore find it difficult to supply themselves with blood. This leads to complications such as diabetic retinopathy and diabetic neuropathy, to diabetic heart disease, and eventually to a significant difficulty in healing wounds and increased risk for Alzheimer's. That is why good oxygenation of the tissues and proper blood and lymph circulation are critical to preserving the health of diabetics. In order to improve blood circulation, I recommend rebounding in place (see Chapter 3) as an extremely important daily exercise. Sprinting in place, powerfully pounding your body (see Chapter 3) and deep and effective breathing (see Chapter 3), alongside light sweating in a sauna and occasional exposure to alternating heat and cold in the shower are effective ways to stimulate the blood circulation.

- Due to diabetics' increased risk for dementia, I recommend performing daily physical activity that involves the brain and demands concentration and attention – folk dancing, ping-pong, playing a musical instrument, tai chi, qigong practices, juggling, dynamic work with a kettlebell, stick play, balance exercises while closing your eyes, spontaneous movement and more. Remember, these are super-exercises that you will perform for your entire life, and so it is important to persist and to perform them every day, all day. You **must** include exercises that require concentration, coordination and attentiveness. An overweight diabetic must perform all his activity outdoors, and it is best if he does so in full sunlight as much as possible, with direct contact between his feet and the ground. Diabetics suffering from neuropathy in their feet, however, should avoid walking barefoot on ground because of potential injury. Nonetheless, they can still enjoy the advantages of proper stimulation of the nerves in the foot by performing stationary exercises, without walking, on a safe surface such as sandy soil or a lawn in their yard or the park, after they ensure that no danger awaits them; such as sharp objects or blistering hot ground. Fortunately, shoes with a very thin and flexible rubber sole imitating barefoot walking or running are readily available.

Many of my pre-diabetic and diabetic patients completely reversed their situation by performing physical exercises while fasting. Being calorically deprived and training at the same time stresses the body, forcing it to adapt. The body adapts by becoming more efficient in fat burning, by recovering faster and by being more metabolically flexible.

6.3 INFLAMMATORY AUTOIMMUNE DISEASES

Autoimmune diseases are the most common type of diseases today, more than cancer and cardiac diseases, high blood pressure and type-2 diabetes. Over a third of the population will suffer, at some point of their lives, from one or more of a long list of autoimmune diseases including lupus, Crohn's disease, multiple sclerosis, type-1 diabetes, rheumatic arthritis, ulcerative colitis and many many others. These diseases are the medical equivalent of "friendly fire." The immune system that was supposed to protect the body suddenly "goes nuts" and begins to attack and destroy healthy tissue. The attacked site changes from disease to disease: in type-1 diabetes, it is the pancreatic beta cells; in Crohn's and ulcerative colitis, the digestive system is attacked; in multiple sclerosis, it is the nervous system; in rheumatoid arthritis, the assault focuses on the joints; whereas in lupus, all the systems of the body can be harmed - kidneys, joints, heart, blood vessels, the liver, the nervous system, the skin and the lungs. Hashimoto's is also an extremely common autoimmune disease. In this disease, the immune system assaults the thyroid gland resulting in inflammation and a decrease in the production and secretion of its hormones. Hypothyroidism is expressed in fatigue, weight gain, hair loss, cold sensitivity, and a rise in the frequency of cardiac diseases, diabetes and cancer. Autoimmune diseases are representative of environmental maladaptation. How can this conflict or discord be reduced or managed? Physical activity should be a part of the strategy to reduce environmental maladaptation. Thus, for Hashimoto's disease, the most common cause of hypothyroidism, vigorous physical activity will lead the cells of the body to be more sensitive to the hormones still secreted by the gland. I had in my clinic quite a few amateur athletes whose blood tests indicated thyroid gland impairment and significant inflammation, but who did not feel the effects. In contrast, even the lightest impairment and inflammation in other, sedentary patients were sufficient enough to result in chronic fatigue and severe obesity. Maintaining mental calm also has a very important role in autoimmune diseases. The immune system tends to be more balanced when we are calm. In scientific jargon, it is common to say that the immune system is more balanced and functions better when we enjoy para-sympathetic tonus, meaning that the parasympathetic nerves work well and save energy by decreasing blood pressure, slowing one's pulse and starting digestion. In this condition, the immune system can calmly devote itself to regular maintenance. That is why any stress-relieving technique is of great aid for dealing with autoimmune diseases. Rebounding, hanging, deep breaths, and qigong exercises immediately place the body in a calmer parasympathetic tonus. As I explained in Chapter 3, rebounding is the best exercise to circulate the blood and lymph and therefore helps prevent the lymphatic system from clogging up.

Controlled exposure to the sun and to cold will also help in nurturing an anti-inflammatory environment. Swimming in cold water, for example, has been found to reduce the inflammatory response in the body, and thereby occasionally halt the progression of autoimmune diseases.

Ice cold showers in the morning can serve as an alternative to swimming or bathing in chilly water. Avoiding artificial electromagnetic radiation as much as possible and having direct contact with the ground are essential to combating autoimmune diseases. I always recommend trying pure, fresh, and local nutrition and attempting to avoid dairy and gluten products for several months to see how the body will respond.

6.4 MENTAL ILLNESSES

Depression, anxiety and even delusions are normal occurrences in everyone's life cycle. However, when they are prolonged and result in suffering, they are classified as mental illnesses or psychiatric disturbances. Psychiatry is currently dominated by the pharmacological approach. This approach treats mental illnesses with powerful drugs which influence the brain, medications such as Prozac and the like, medications such as Valium and Clonazepam, Seroquel (Quetiapine) and Risperidone, and others. Like every branch of medicine, the psychiatric approach is therapeutic rather than preventive. That is why we see throughout the Western World a constant rise in the frequency of all mental illnesses. Psychiatric medications are notorious for their questionable safety profile and the endless list of side effects associated with them. Drugs such as SSRIs (selective serotonin reuptake inhibitors), for example, can result in a decline in libido, obesity, and addiction. Taking them over many years can result in full-blown depression. Risperidone almost always results in obesity and increased blood sugar levels. All sedatives from the benzodiazepine family are packed with dangerous side effects such as falling, depression, addiction and more. We could live with these side effects if these drugs really helped everyone significantly, but recent studies show that the benefits of SSRI medication, for example, is miniscule at most.

One of the primary factors in the constant rise of depression prevalence is the absence of physical activity. Other important factors are: insufficient exposure to sunlight that leads to a type of depression known as seasonal affective disorder (SAD); inflammatory autoimmune diseases (such as rheumatism and celiac); hypothyroidism (extremely common in women); nutritional deficiencies (such as low vitamin B12 levels, low magnesium, niacin or omega-3 fatty acid); exposure to environmental toxins (such as lead and mercury); head injuries; mental trauma from the past; chronic viral infections; imbalance of intestinal flora; lack of sleep; chronic stress; various medications (such as beta blockers, interferon and more); disruption of the biological clock; disruption of hormonal signaling (a common situation in postnatal depression); continual exposure to blue light; and social isolation.

Unfortunately, most psychiatrists, internal medicine practitioners and family doctors skip right over these underlying factors and rush immediately at the synthetic molecules or medications that, of course, completely disregard these diverse factors. To truly recover from depression, one must review each of the possible causes and consider how much of an effect it has on the patient. Usually, there are several coexisting factors responsible for depression. This makes the task complex, but its advantage is that any solution generated is free of side effects and will truly help the patient achieve a sustainable recovery. To heal the internal movement of the brain, one must concurrently ensure proper and wise external movement by the body. Many studies have shown that physical activity is an extremely effective means of treating any type of mental imbalance.

Here are a few exercises I recommend for handling mental imbalance:

- Rebounding (see Chapter 3) - this is the number one exercise for mental imbalance. Many patients suffering from depression sometimes find it hard to even rise from their bed, and certainly cannot perform a full exercise. Instead, they can hop on the bed, next to the bed, or wherever they may be. The harmonic and uniform jumping movement creates a harmonic and uniform movement in the brain for at least a few seconds. If one repeats a brief interval of jumping for 10-20 seconds several times a day, the brain can literally be forced into balance. The shaking motion of the body during the rebound stimulates lymph circulation and helps balance any inflammatory situation in the body. While rebounding, the individual is in control of powerful and stable bodily movement. The rapid movement of the rebound also awakens the brain, which can be rather drowsy due to depression or the use of medications.

- Hanging bar - hanging from a pull-up bar (see Chapter 3) is an excellent para-sympathetic exercise. It is excellent for anyone in high sympathetic tonus or, in other words, people suffering from anxiety.

- All-out activity (see Chapter 3) - recruits internal mental reserves. It forces us to make a massive effort for a brief, survival-stimulating interval. Extreme survival situations are known to immediately cancel out almost any mental illness (save extreme cases of schizophrenia). You will not be able to distinguish, for example, between a depressed individual and a healthy one when they are fleeing a bear who has gotten free of its cage in the zoo. When an individual is in an all-out-like situation, the conditions override his entire personality structure; thoughts, emotions, sensations, medical and/or social condition. Everything is completely devoted to one goal and one goal only – giving his all to survive. These all-out activities simulate hunting or flight and require the immediate mobilization of brain resources, thereby training the nervous system towards this goal. Repeating these activities daily will protect a person from mental conditions such as depression and help those conditions fade away more rapidly. Any all-out exercise is good, particularly short sprints in place and sudden exposure to cold water in the pool, ocean, or shower.

- Breathing exercises - when a person is under stress or feels anxious, the breath grows shallow and ineffective, leading to yawning and moaning, and desperate attempts at deeper breaths to compensate for the feeling of insufficient air. Exercises involving very long breaths, such as qigong exercises (see Chapter 3) can be extremely helpful. The Wim Hof breathing exercises (see Chapter 3) are an excellent way to release endorphins and dopamine and immediately feel a lift in your mood. When an ice-cold shower is added immediately thereafter, you benefit from an additional immediate improvement to your mood. Practicing breath exercises can be a gamechanger for anxious and depressed patients and I think it should be an integral part of treating such patients.

- Facial exercises - the facial muscles are closest to the brain and are therefore the first to absorb and reflect our mood. I therefore recommend performing a variety of facial exercises for several minutes, and particularly smiling exercises (see Chapter 3) daily. Studies have shown that when we smile even an artificial smile, the brain releases the same beneficial molecules secreted as when we smile naturally.

- Coordination exercises - these exercises require the brain to work in harmony with the body and with precision, so the brain can soothe the body when it operates chaotically and is out of balance. Any qigong or kettlebell exercise are good for this purpose, as are any other series of actions that are to be performed precisely.

- Awareness of the "depressed" posture versus a "happy" posture - since depression is associated with a slouched posture and a downturned mouth, it is very important to perform exercises that straighten our posture throughout the day, repeatedly, if only for a few seconds. These leads our body to be more erect and deepen our breathing.

Aside from physical activity, additional activities scientifically proven to aid in treating depression and anxiety are spending time in nature, working in the garden, staring at a forest, walking barefoot on the ground and swimming in the ocean. Furthermore, physical contact is extraordinarily effective for improving these conditions. Many people who suffer from mental illnesses are in a state of social isolation. Often, the social isolation is the cause of the depression, whereas in other cases it is the result. Social isolation is a complex and difficult issue to treat (one cannot stuff friends and families into a pill). The quickest way to slightly ameliorate its devastating effects is through bodily contact. The very touch of skin on skin immediately make us feel better, whether the skin is that of another person, an animal, or ourselves. I recommend for anyone suffering from a troubling emotional state to orient themselves towards daily contact with skin, hug as much as possible, undergo massage treatments, adopt an animal, and even touch their own skin. Daily self-touching by powerful pounding on the body (the gorilla exercise) or by gentle massage of the face and body, or gentle stroking of the body as part of the qigong exercises, will greatly improve our inner feeling of health.

6.5 PROBLEMS WITH LIBIDO AND SEXUAL FUNCTION

Erectile dysfunction and decline in libido and are the nightmare of every man. The question is not whether it will happen, but when and for how long. Studies have clearly indicated that testosterone levels have declined over the past generation in every age group. The reasons for this are unclear, but there are several leading candidates, including absence of physical activity, reduced muscle mass, obesity, prolonged sitting, chronic stress and sugary foods.

So how can this problem be handled?

The animal exercises offer some unexpected aids. These exercises, in which we imagine that we are an animal, awaken our animal instinct:

- Power pose - an interesting study has shown that we can raise our testosterone levels by 20 percent and reduce our cortisol levels via assuming the "power pose." In the power pose, we swell and enlarge our body, just as many animals do: puff out your chest and pound it vigorously, stand with one leg extended forward, place your body weight on the back leg, swing your arms forward with your fingers curved like cat paws, and stretch with your arms straight and drawn to the sides, and your head lifted.

I recommend that you watch the TED talk of the social psychologist Amy Cuddy from 2012, "Fake it Till You Make It."

- Exercises to loosen up and move the pelvis - the wave exercise and the hand dance exercise are excellent for moving the pelvis and causing blood to circulate in that area. The wave exercise simulates a penetrative pelvis movement, and hence loosens up and trains all muscles of the pelvis.
- Massage - daily massage with a roller helps relieve muscle stress from the pelvic area.
- Muscle strengthening - increasing muscle volume via strength exercises raises testosterone levels throughout the body. Pull-ups and daily exercise with the kettlebell, accompanied by several isometric exercises, will rapidly expand the muscle mass, provided

they are performed daily in short intervals. Traditional work with weights in the gym is good and effective to fulfill this need as well.

- Animal exercises are excellent to connect to our primal, animalistic side. Even a few seconds of bear walks, monkey walks, pounding on your chest like a gorilla or doing frog leaps have the ability to invigorate the body and the mind.

- Try to avoid prolonged bike riding, for this tends to place excessive pressure on the prostate and may numb the nerve bundles in the area.

CHAPTER 7

Fascia tissue? What is that?

One of the charming questions coming from Jonathan, my youngest son who just turned four, is "What's that?", asked in a sweet, high voice filled with typical, child-like astonishment. I get an identical response, just in a deeper voice, from both patients and doctors when I talk about the importance of the fascia's health. Fascia is composed of collagen fibers that connect all our tissues to each other, from head to tiptoes. It forms a surface similar to a fishnet stocking to which every muscle in the body is interlinked. Fascia layers surround and pack each of the muscles in our body, providing them with shape and form. Gentler layers of fascia are also present in each of the muscles and are similar in shape to the gentle layer separating the segments of an orange. The fascia layers surrounding the muscle are transformed at its end to tendons that connect the muscle to the bone. Collagen fibers link the muscle along its entire length to the bone, and tiny fibers of collagen are also present between our cells, providing structure and support to the blood vessels, the lymphatic fluid capillaries, and the nerves passing through them. Collagen fibers envelop all of the blood vessels thus creating their basic structure and round form. Different patterns of collagen fibers create the bones, tendons, cartilage and disks. In fact, the fascia and collagen fibers are interwoven within each organ and cell of our bodies.

The fascia also contains a few elastin fibers which provide the skin, muscles and blood vessels with their characteristic flexibility and elasticity, as well as sugar composites (glycosaminoglycans) whose role is to store water around them, enabling the fascia to move smoothly and without friction. One of the primary sugar formations is hyaluronic acid, which is commonly injected into joints under conditions of osteoarthritis, and in aesthetic medicine to the facial skin in order to fill in wrinkles. The collagen fibers are the building blocks of the fascia tissue. The fiber itself is a protein constructed of long amino acid chains. Imagine a string of pearls stretching out in a straight line; each pearl is a single amino acid, and every string or chain contains 400 pearls. Three such chains bind to one another just like a braid, in a three-dimensional structure called a triple helix. The length of such a collagen molecule is 300 nanometers. A cluster of collagen molecules forms a collagen fiber. The collagen fibers, depending on their spatial arrangement, density, and interaction with other collagen fibers and molecules, form the various fascia formations and collagen types. (There are 28 types, but Type I is the most common in the body.)

Until recently, scientists and doctors believed that the fascia and collagen fibers serve as no more than biological glue. However, over the past few years, several research groups, particularly in Germany, began studying the fascia itself both under the microscope and during muscle activity, and what they discovered is nothing short of amazing. It turns out that nearly half of the power we produce derives from the activity of the fascia itself and not, as was commonly thought, from the contraction and release of the muscle. The fascia operates in many cases like an elastic spring that knows how to store and release energy. The cells producing the collagen, called fibroblasts are very much influenced by hormones and many other molecules, such as inflammation mediators. Furthermore, the fascia contains many nerves. This very effectively clarifies the connection between body and mind, for chronic mental stress results in the secretion of stress hormones such as adrenalin and cortisol, and these in turn cause the fascia to contract and thicken and slowly lose its ability to move smoothly and flexibly. That is why a high percentage of those suffering from depression also suffer from chronic back pain. Chronic back pain is very common in the general population with an entire entourage of orthopedic surgeons, roentgen specialist, physiotherapists, acupuncturists, osteopaths, chiropractors, masseuses, and of course a whole plethora of pain-countering medications such as Voltaren, Arcoxia, Tramadol, Percocet, Morphine epidural injections and so forth. The classical medical thinking refers to two primary causes of back pain; spastic and inflamed muscles, and disk herniation which press upon the nerves. There are other, rarer factors such as are the narrowing of the spinal cord, cancerous growth or metastatic secondary growth, fractures and more. However, study of the fascia tissue indicates that it is the root cause of most back pain, both chronic and acute, as well as chronic pain in the shoulders, elbows, neck and elsewhere.

When the fascia tissue is impaired, it shrinks and weakens, the nerve cells within it begin broadcasting pain. The fascia can be impaired by absence of motion as well as prolonged sitting or unstable posture, by chronic dehydration (very common in the modern age), by other inflammatory processes (including autoimmune diseases), or sudden loads that result in tears. The fascia can also be impaired by the following: mental stress, leading it to respond with calcification, shrinkage and thickening; deficient nutrition that fails to provide it with sufficient building blocks for maintenance; or weakened vision that changes the body posture.

Just like the rest of our body, the fascia is subject to aging. The collagen fiber networks lose their elasticity, dry up, grow rigid, thicken, calcify, stick to one another, and eventually weaken and lead to cellulite, osteoporosis, wrinkles, joint pains, rigid movements and endless other negative side effects. There exists a perverse feedback loop in which pain from the deterioration of the fascia reduces movement, which in turn further harms the health of the fascia. Harm to the organization and function of the collagen fibers will also, as mentioned previously, harm the blood vessels and lymph vessels that pass through them. Harm to the fascia quality is what actually inflicts an "aged" appearance and feeling on our body.

Luckily, contemporary research indicates that we can largely influence the health of our fascia and considerably slow down its deterioration

What exercises can help preserve our connective tissues?

1. **Rebounding** - to preserve the elastic springlike quality of the fascia, one should perform a daily brief set of rebounding exercises (see Chapter 3). My experience with patients is that any type of rebounding is good. With time, aim for slightly higher and more powerful rebounds. It is enough to count between two and four powerful and high jumps a day. Those who have not jumped in many years should begin with light rebounding, with only slight lifting of the heels. A study published in 2015 in the European Journal of Applied Physiology examines the influence of rebounding on the fascia of 20 older participants. The researchers discovered a considerable improvement in many parameters, such as jumping height, the quality of their Achilles tendon, the quality of their ankle joints and more.

2. **Stretching exercises** - the fascia tissue loves slow, relaxed stretching with diversification of angles and various loads. Basic stretches such as bending with your hands to the floor, stretching upwards or various yoga positions cause the fascia to expand and contract and enable it to receive a fresh supply of blood. Methods such as

yoga, tai chi, qigong, Pilates or Feldenkrais are very soothing and generate a hormonal environment which relaxes the fascia.

3. **Massage** - one can also soothe the fascia with the foam roller (see Chapter 3) just like dough. Daily use for several minutes of the roller does wonders for the fascia. Beginners are recommended to skip the lower back region. The roller enables us to perform massage-like work on ourselves. Deep tissue massage, suction cups, shiatzu, Rolfing, myofascial release and various other alternative medicine methods are good as well, but they tend to be less accessible.

4. **Perfect posture stance** - fascia is, to a large extent, like putty. It is shaped by the way we move, breathe, eat and sleep. That is why, at least once a day, I recommend returning to a perfect posture and reminding the fascia how it is supposed to behave when the body is calm, relaxed, erect and loose but ready for action. Rebounding, gentle stretches, massaging with a foam roller and standing in our perfect posture constitute the four components of daily fascia support and cultivation. Daily exercise of these four components should constitute the basis of our movement, for the fascia is the basis of our entire physical structure. These are extremely simple and highly available exercises; they are very easy on the body and therefore appropriate for any age. I recommend repeating it several times a day. Every day. All of your life.

CHAPTER 8

Motivation, flow, potential

Physical activity begins and ends in our mind. Our mind is what determines every parameter of activity – to do or not to do, what activity to perform, for how long, at what intensity, and where to perform the activity. The brain also determines the strength and coordination of the movement. We tend to admire the ballerina's grace and Schwarzenegger's muscles, but their common secret is the strength of their mental ability.

In this chapter we will try to understand how the mind can skillfully recruit itself to support and boost physical activity.

Below are a few examples of the dramatic role the mind played in physical activity and what happened when it is fully mobilized to the task:

1. 1953: Sir Edmund Hillary is the first man to reach the top of Mount Everest.
2. 1954: Roger Bannister is the first individual to run a mile in under four minutes.
3. 1996: Kerri Strug is the Olympic gymnast whose performance determined if the United States Olympic Team would outmatch the Soviet one. In the pommel horse exercise, she landed imperfectly and limped away on a badly sprained ankle. Nonetheless, she

returned for her second attempt which she performed flawlessly before collapsing on the mattress, and brought the gold for her team.

4. 2005: Danny Way, one of the greatest skateboarders in history, attempted to jump over the Great Wall of China using a mega ramp built especially for him. In his first training jump he fractured his ankle and tore an internal ligament in his knee. Twenty-four hours later, with 125 million Chinese following him on television, he slowly climbed up 10 stories and retried the jump. He succeeded, and then repeated the jump four more times.

5. 2015: Ninety-five-year-old Charles Eugster shattered the world record for the 200-meter dash for 95-year-olds and above. He completes the sprint in 55 seconds.

Let us see if we mere mortals can also reach the mental state of these successful athletes.

But what is this mental state?

The American-Hungarian psychologist Mihaly Csikszentmihalyi studied the mental condition characterizing the peak experiences of athletes, artists, musicians and also of "regular" people. He recognized a specific concept that he coined "flow" and the following list highlights the characteristics of this notion:

1. A task which requires absolute concentration in its performance – it is highly desirable for this mission to be clear and have clear goals.

2. A challenging task which requires the activation of specific skills to face the challenge – it is important not to make the challenge too difficult in order to avoid frustration, but also not too easy so as to prevent boredom.

3. Immediate feedback in regard to success or failure – failure has

a cost such as a painful fall, loss in a competition, a false musical note, or a low grade.

4. Feeling of control and ownership over the mission – in accordance to the feedback, one can change an attitude immediately in order to better succeed next time.

5. A significant change in the perception of time – an hour can fly by without noticing and one completely loses track of time.

6. Conscious thoughts and self-reflection disappear – one cannot navigate down a stormy river and at the same time think about career or work problems, or anything else for that matter, for conscious thoughts disturb concentration, and the cost of such an error can be quite high.

7. Outside needs are pushed aside and the experience fills one's entire existence.

8. The environment is complex and unexpected, which leads one to focus even more on the mission (think of the snowy slope of a mountain).

Today, we know that the "flow" condition is characterized by simultaneous release of no less than five neural mediators; norepinephrine, dopamine, anandamide, endorphins and serotonin. The brain is fueled by these five neural mediators which create a highly addictive experience that we wish to return to again and again. This sounds like addiction – but this is the best aspect of addiction, otherwise known as motivation. The desire to return to the flow state generates an internal motivation to practice and repeat the actions leading to this situation, whether it is competing in a chess tournament, conducting an orchestra, performing skateboard tricks, juggling five balls, or solving a problem successfully at work.

Surprisingly, the flow state shuts off parts of our brain. The prefrontal lobe, the one responsible for self-consciousness, the sense of self, internal criticism and the sense of time, switches off. The brain transitions to a more subconscious state, known as "the deep now." In this state, the willingness to take risks rises, the internal critic falls silent, pains vanish, and the human potential flourishes.

It is therefore not surprising that studies performed by Csikszent-mihalyi and other researchers indicated that people who know how to enter this state on a regular basis are happier, less depressed and anxious, tend to have a higher education and income and get divorced less often. The reason for the rise in pleasure and the decline in pain is the endorphins secreted during the flow condition. That is why people suffering from pain, particularly in third age, are recommended to enter this state as often as possible. Daily physical activity with flow characteristics therefore constitutes a truly splendid way to combat illnesses and various pains.

Flow, in its full power, occurs when the level of our skills is very high, and the challenge level is very high as well. In the flow state, along with peak physical capabilities, we learn more quickly, remember better, and are also far more creative. In contrast, apathy, wariness, anxiety, and boredom are a sign that we are not in a flow state. For example, watching television, randomly surfing the web, or using the treadmill while staring at a screen require no skills whatsoever and hence do not pose any personal challenge. Other activities which pose a low challenge and require no skills to perform such as walking, running, or swimming, may bore us at some stage. Of course, such activities are better than nothing, but it is rather hard to generate strong internal motivation to persevere in them.

All of us have experienced flow in one way or another throughout our lives. Some experience it at work: surgeons, pilots, scientists, musicians and authors can "vanish" into their high-concentration work and lose their sense of time, as can carpenters and kindergarten teachers. Children, if they are permitted, tend to easily float into this state of "the deep now" as well.

Place before your child a challenging task like Lego, putting together a puzzle or a game of outdoor tag, and you will realize how he or she easily enters a flow state. The influence of the flow state lasts even after we leave it. Under its influence we are calmer, filled with satisfaction, more concentrated and focused, and the result is that we are already planning for the next time we will enter this state.

This is the strongest inner motivation, and it pushes athletes, musicians, artists and chess masters to repeat their experience again and again, and even to seek to improve their skill levels or the challenge level.

We, too, can learn from extreme sports seekers how to crack the flow state and how to reach it without performing somersaults in the air or leaping over the Great Wall of China. Physical activity is an excellent gateway into the flow state at any age and any skill level. However, to enable us to enter the flow state, the activity must challenge us in some way. It must be performed in a rich and complex environment and be integrated with immediate feedback.

The super-exercise model was designed specifically to render the flow state accessible to people who do not leap from giant ramps or scale Mt. Everest. I very much encourage trainees and patients to place small challenges in their path every day of their lives, and to get used to performing physical activity from a sense of internal challenge, aiming at slightly improving their skills at every opportunity. As you may have understood by now, creativity in new exercises and variations to the training environment are more than welcome. For example, try to rotate a kettlebell around your body. To perform this feat, you must be extremely well focused, otherwise it might fall and perhaps cause harm. This type of activity is already a small challenge which incorporates danger when doing it and, as a result, the brain immediately becomes more concentrated. If we try to perform the exercise more quickly or do more repetitions or vary it, we slightly improve our skills and the brain immediately becomes more engaged. So, over the course of 30-60 seconds, we place ourselves in a state of flow. We can choose to perform the exercise in a more complex environment, say outside in the park and barefoot on the grass. The brain will then be provided with more environmental stimuli and as a result, we immediately become more focused, the challenge level rises, and we enter a flow state. any exercise which requires balance , like qi qong exercises or rebounding pushes the brain to a higher level of concentration. If we perform the exercise with eyes shut, an element of uncertainty and danger which leads the brain to further concentrate and enter a flow state, is added to this heady brew.

When we try to break our personal record with push-ups, a difficult challenge is formed, and with it also internal motivation to improve. Juggling exercises, walking on a tightrope, animal exercises and various rebounding exercises are additional ways to immediately enter a flow state, and so are hobbies such as folk dancing, ball games, and of course any extreme sport. I also recommend you never give up on a hobby that immerses you in a flow state because of schedule constraints or because of your age.

In the third age, the last thing you should do is give up a rich and complex environment. The trick the 95-year-old Charles Eugster used was to register into an international contest. There is nothing like an upcoming competition to infuse interest and super-motivation into your daily training. There is nothing like a new stadium and new contestants to create a rich and stimulating environment.

We do not cease playing because we grow old. We grow old because we cease playing.

Children love to move their bodies. They quite naturally like to run, play, jump and climb. Over the years, we grow older, our physical fitness changes, our body changes and we have other seemingly more important priorities. Nonetheless, it is crucially important to preserve the energy of playfulness and the flow state until our dying breath.

An excellent example of this is the Canadian Olga Kotelko, whose standard life story received a dramatic turn when she decided to start competing in track and field events at the age of 77! She passed away in 2014 at the age of 95, and by then had won hundreds of medals and broken dozens of world records for her age group. ("Masters" competitions include different age groups, with separate brackets for every five years; 70-75, 75-80, and so forth.)

In his excellent book "What Makes Olga Run?: The Mystery of the 90-Something Track Star and What She Can Teach Us About Living Longer, Happier Lives," (Henry Holt; 2014,) the author Bruce Grierson took Olga to a sports lab. She underwent a muscle biopsy there to discover whether there were any genetic characteristics that might explain the 90-year-old's astounding athletic performances. It seems that her results were quite average, and after a battery of psychological tests, Grierson concluded that her magic was in her extraordinary mental attitude, not her ordinary body. She placed goals, documented her results in the diary and was an open and loving woman. (The Yiddishism which Grierson employs is "mensch.")

In studies performed on people who compete in Masters Tournaments (such as Hastings et al., 1995), researchers mention several reasons that push these individuals to continue to compete and train in their advanced age. Some of the reasons include setting personal goals, improved health, the desire to be fit, the desire to improve their skills, enjoyment, and contact with other trainees and contestants. In another study, researchers surveyed 610 long-distance runners and found that women emphasized the desire to reduce their weight, psychological coping, a purpose in life and self-esteem (Ogles et al., 1995).

Many elderly athletes know that over the years we all lose physical, mental and social capabilities. That is why, as the study shows, a common mantra they tend to utter is "use it or lose it" (Dionigi, 2007). The desire to cope with the aging process, slow it down and postpone it while maintaining a good quality of life, very much characterizes the oldest group of athletes.

One of the goals of the super-exercise training model is to reach the third age in peak physical condition, and to continue to improve thereafter. This in and of itself is a phenomenal challenge, in which men and women pit themselves against entropy itself. When we push ourselves, we immediately color our activity with a very important aspect of the flow state – facing a challenge.

In his book "50 Athletes over 50: Teach Us to Live a Strong, Healthy Life," (Wise Media Group, 2010) author Don McGrath notes that elderly athletes generally recount four pleasures that motivate them to persist in sports:

- Pleasure from movement; elderly athletes successfully preserve their childlike playfulness and thereby enjoy physical activity.
- Pleasure from achievements; elderly athletes come to terms with the change in their performance over the years and find new challenges in every age.
- Enjoyment from optimal health. Young athletes often literally ruin their bodies in order to win competitions. In contrast, older athletes enjoy better health than their age peers, which spurs them on to continue.
- Pleasure in social connections with other athletes.

McGrath found that athletes over 50 are divided into three main groups. The first group includes people who were always physically active; the second includes people who were physically active in their youth, stopped at some point and returned to activity at an older age; and the third group includes athletes that had only begun to seriously exercise at an older age and had never been physically active. In other words, it is never too late to start with enjoyable physical activity. We all want to enter the third age healthy and strong, as well as happy, socially networked, and productively and engagingly employed.

Regular physical activity is an excellent way to significantly slow down the aging process and preserve the qualities of health, strength and joy. So what should those who currently have no motivation or reason to persist in physical activity and do not know how to enter the flow state do?

Here are my recommendations:

- Form habits and self-discipline. Commit to a single exercise over 10-20 seconds once or twice a day, just like brushing your teeth, thereby training your self-discipline muscle as well.
- Occasionally, especially during physical workout, try to break down old habits and try something new. Combining old habits with new activities is the basis for success and creativity.
- Place before you challenges and goals on a daily or weekly basis. I recommend writing down or drawing up the goals in order to succeed, and managing a diary where you can unload everything on your mind onto paper. Keeping a diary and writing are very effective ways of achieving goals and internal psychological relief.
- Compete in a specific sport, or join a team that will constantly motivate you.
- Look at life from the perspective of a child who just wants to play. In other words, lighten up and chill out. Physical activity is an invitation to play, move your body and release tension.
- Always strive to improve. An internal feeling of progress and a desire to be more skilled, stronger, quicker, and generally just "more" are very powerful motivational engines.
- Imagine yourselves as incredibly old but very healthy and vigorous,

providing an outstanding personal example to your children, grandchildren and great grandchildren. I suggest to my patients to imagine themselves jumping as limberly as they are doing right now, decades in the future when they are 80 or 90.

- Tap into inspirational sources. Today in the internet age, it is easy to find books, videos and YouTube clips about people who have succeeded in various fields. The aphorism is that success leaves tracks. Find the tracks left by successful people and they will help you and provide you with the push you need to succeed.

- Develop "antibodies" to depression, anxiety, apathy, fatigue, and burnout. Antibodies such as a strong spiritual belief system, a purpose in life, volunteering, nurturing social interconnectedness, high-quality sleep and balanced nutrition, and therapy if necessary.

- Start now. Make a change for the better in your lifestyle and behavioral patterns, including your physical activity patterns. This is something you should start on right now, regardless of your age. I can assure you that the benefit is an excellent chance for successful and graceful aging. SET makes it possible for everyone to start right here, right now. All you need to do is perform one super-exercise a day for a few seconds and slowly, at your own pace improve and expand your practice.

CHAPTER 9

Super-Exercise Training for Amateur Athletes

A very small part of the population performs regular, intensive and prolonged physical activity. Beyond good-to-excellent physical fitness, athletes typically tend to share a certain mental attitude. They love to move and very much love their sports hobbies – a love that can sometimes reach addiction-like levels, and which generates a strong motivation to move and train. This motivation, determination, persistence and willingness to persevere exists in spite of difficulties we all encounter; boredom, physical pain, injury, lack of time and laziness. Athletes are also characterized by high self-discipline, which is expressed in the adoption of a healthy lifestyle. Junk food, smoking, alcohol, drugs, and too little sleep can impair athletic capabilities. The type of athletic field or hobby is secondary to the mental state. Super-exercise training several times each day may seem like a joke to an athlete. The brief time devoted to every exercise combined with its ease and simplicity are intended, among other purposes, to get those lacking in motivation, determination and persistence, to move wisely and well, whereas athletes have no motivational problems. On the contrary, professional and amateur athletes oftentimes suffer from exactly the opposite problem. The athlete is used to long, grueling training. He counts the time of the training in hours, whereas I count it in seconds and minutes. Nonetheless, I also advise athletes, at any point in their lives, to incorporate the performance of super-exercises for several seconds to minutes each day.

There are several good reasons to do so:

- The super-exercises include movements we will want to preserve throughout our entire life. At a certain age, we will be faced with the challenges of biological aging such as weaker muscles, chronic diseases, medications, and accumulated injuries, which unfortunately do not spare even elite athletes. That is why most athletes abandon their hobbies over the years. You will not find many 60-year-olds playing soccer three times a week or snowboarding daily. And when the hobby is gone, most athletes become mere mortals. They cease training, or else limit their exercises to a few typical "blocks" such as walking on the treadmill. S., one of my patients, was in an elite army unit. Like many discharged veterans, he turned to running to keep fit. However, over the past few years, almost without noticing, S. had downshifted and running almost completely evaporated from his life. Boredom reduced his activity level. The divorce from the mother of his children was the deathblow. He had performed no physical activity over the last three years, even in the gym located in the building where he lives. He simply felt too tired and lazy to train. I meet many such people in his condition in the clinic. I call it the "past glory syndrome." When I ask them what physical activity they perform today, they tell me instead of their military or athletic exploits 30 years ago. The sixth decade presents a difficult mental wall for most athletes. Intensity drops, and only the truly mentally strong and determined survive this decade. The super-exercise model was designed to enable us to perform wise, good, and daily movement regardless of our mental state. Through the super-exercise training, the athlete maintains an intimate, daily connection with his body, and optimally prepares it for the third age.

- The super-exercises fill any type of training gap; injury, lack of time, laziness, and weather. Lack of time is a very significant problem for athletes who are parents to children and who simultaneously manage a challenging career. Daily practice of wise and good movements in short bouts will preserve the abilities and stamina of the athlete during the pressured periods in which he or she lacks sufficient time for intensive training and will enable him to continue to enjoy his hobby.

- SET is a perfectly suited for people with great athletic potential like adolescents or young people in their first decades who are not drawn to any specific traditional sport or hobby. My oldest son is seventeen years old. Like many of his friends he was not drawn to any particular sport activity and began spending more and more time glued to various screens. Two years ago he started, of his own volition, to play with super-exercises. He did not read my book, nor did I guide him or encourage him in any way. He simply saw, over the years, how I engaged my body. He was particularly drawn to bodyweight classical exercises. He started doing push-ups, squats and pull-ups. He was training without any trainer and without any program or set times. He would start a training session when he felt like it and stop after a while when he got tired or bored or had something better to do. Later, when he grew stronger, he started challenging himself with more and more difficult exercises and flirting with his comfort zone. As of the time of this writing, he has become quite a beast. He is doing one-handed push-ups, he is doing a front lever, he is doing Olympic rings muscle-ups (an exercise that even I struggle with), and he is doing handstands. He also started wall climbing and has become quite good at it.

Because his motivation grew organically from within and because he directly experienced the benefits of a strong and supple body, there is a good chance that he will maintain this level of fitness throughout his life.

- Super-exercises support any athletic hobby and enable its maintenance over years to come. A healthy connective tissue, properly trained, enables good movement in any type of athletic hobby. That is why fascia exercises and qigong exercises will support any activity whatsoever. A diverse all-body workout to strengthen your muscles with kettlebells and performance of isometric all-out exercises will support any activity type and enable its persistence in later ages. So it is that I, at the age of 55, can still freely and pleasurably ride my skateboard and perform cool exercises like board slides, 50-50 grinds and many more, and still wave surf with ease performing of the lips and the like. Through my daily super-exercise training, I retain the elastic suppleness of my connective tissue and preserve a proper and stable muscle envelope around my joints.
- Any type of super-exercises can, with a little extra investment of time and effort, become an athletic hobby in and of itself. The pull-up bar alone can provide athletic occupation for life, as can skipping rope, doing classic exercises or qigong. Combining two or more groups of super-exercises can enable you to reach a very high intensity. When a diverse and highly intensive exercise of even a few seconds is performed daily for years, it enables us to enjoy an excellent basic fitness. For example, at the end of a work-packed day, and after an evening filled with a pile of squealing children, when you don't have the energy to go out for a run or do another intensive exercise, this is precisely the time and the place to perform a set of pull-ups and push-ups in an all-out style, a few athletic rebounds in place, several stretches, and a few squats. You

can repeat this array twice. A well-trained amateur athlete can reach 20 pull-ups and 50 push-ups, and together with the other exercises, he wins five super-intensive minutes in which he has exercised every component of physical activity.

In the following clip I demonstrate the evolution of 40 years of pull up bar training. In about 40 seconds I perform powerful athletic jumps from bar to bar.

Many fit adults do block/box sports like jogging, swimming, triathlon, lifting weights, yoga, and Pilates. What is missing from their routines is the playful, creative, and childlike state of mind. SET makes this state of mind accessible to everybody through spontaneous movement, facial exercises, rebounding variations, and playing with the kettlebell rather than doing a predetermined number of reps. These super-exercises are techniques to engage the mind-body continuum in loose and refreshing ways.

- One of the terms which defines an athlete is repetitions or reps. The athlete repeats certain movements again and again to become better, faster, stronger and more skillful. A professional basketball player will shoot the ball thousands upon thousands of times to perfect his shot, a bodybuilder will lift weights thousands of times, and a marathon runner will run and run and run in his quest to be as fit as he can be.

Repetitions, though, come with a price. They inevitably lead to wear and tear, injuries, and eventual physical and mental blockage of the athlete. Athletes should always diversify their training if they want to stay fit for their entire lives. SET offers the athlete many ways in which he or she can engage in exercising without endless repetitions and with infinite variations of his daily training — refreshing variations that are injury- and boredom-proof.

- The super-exercise model includes breathing exercises. Athletes tend to take breathing for granted. They simply inhale and exhale vigorously during practice and that is that. But dedicated breathing practice can deeply influence athletic ability and help with rapid recovery after training. I lack the space to go into greater detail here about how you should practice your breathing. I have practiced the Wim Hof breathing method and play the didgeridoo almost daily. Whenever I go on my daily errands, I do box breaths or breath holds. Other breathing exercises are detailed in Chapter 3.

Over the years, the aging process leads to reduction in lung volume and breathing effectiveness, a decline which harms athletic abilities, and which can result in a negative feedback loop of declining activity leading to increased breathing impairment and so on. Breathing exercises focus solely on the lungs and the surrounding bones and muscles, and are extremely effective in preserving healthy breathing for years to come.

After training, a calm breathing exercise soothes the body and transitions it from a state of high adrenaline to relaxation and recovery mode.

- The super-exercise model provides the amateur athlete a chance to protect himself from injury and occupy his body when he is recovering from injuries. Injuries are an inescapable part of the life of every athlete. Intensity and flirting with danger take their toll, always and without exception. Any amateur athlete will reach 40-50 with several injuries racked up, which he mostly still feels. In fact, from the sixth decade onwards, the measure of the amateur athlete (there are no more professional athletes at this age, other than gym and ski instructors), is in how he copes and recovers from stretched, cramped and torn muscles, as well as bleeding, inflammation and fractures. Use of the foam roller, qigong exercises, strength exercises with kettlebells, animal exercises among others SET techniques preserve the connective tissue, the muscles and keep the brain active and synchronized with the body. I particularly recommend making the acquaintance of the isometric exercise group, which enables exercising over wounded, and even cast-encased, portions of your body.

Many athletes will crash into a physical and mental wall in their sixth decade, if not earlier . The aging process is accompanied by social obligations such as family, career, friends, and so on. Navigating through this age and still preserving athletic fitness is challenging, to say the least. Being an old athlete requires mastery in areas other than moving the body safely and efficiently.

I found the following modalities to support my athleticism and help me to stay in the game 100%:

- Cold exposure – As a Wim Hof method trainer (see Chapter 3), I am used to taking cold showers each day, particularly after intensive physical activity. Cold showers are a well-known way of dealing with muscle aches and light injuries post-training. An amateur athlete can immediately begin to shower in cold water and swim or bathe in the ocean when it is cold. By contending with the chilly temperature, the body upgrades its anti-inflammatory abilities. Dealing with cold also works on our mental state and can make us more determined, mentally strong, healthier and happier. If you want to take cold exposure to the next level, you can immerse yourself in ice-cold water. In Israel, naturally icy cold water is hard to find year round, so I bought a big freezer, filled it with water and turned it into a frosty 2-3 Celsius ice-water bath (approximately 36.5 F) available for use no matter the season.
- Fasts – Fasts are ancient methods making a comeback thanks to scientific studies that have revealed just how efficient they are in supporting our overall health and longevity. Fasts, like extreme cold or heat, place survival stress on the body. To cope with this pressure, the body activates genetic backup programs that are dormant when we stay in our comfort zone. These programs upgrade our immune system, making us more resistant to inflammation. Physical activity performed during fasting (drinking water, tea

or coffee in unlimited amounts is permitted) forces our body to produce energy more efficiently (simulating a hunter seeking his prey on an empty stomach) by increasing the number and quality of the intracellular organelles responsible for generating energy (the mitochondria). In short, proper recovery is enhanced in the fasting state. Fasting as a way of life is the best safeguard against the ominous weight gains that tend to materialize out of nowhere as we grow older. When we fast for 24 hours or more, the body begins to literally eat itself up, a process called autophagy. In its wisdom, the body starts with the weak and cancerous cells before it turns on the healthy cells. Furthermore, fasting seems to be the best way to spur the generation of new stem cells, which makes it an excellent anti-aging strategy. I and many other accomplished athletes around the world practice intermittent fasting, skipping breakfasts, and training on empty stomach. I took it one step further and, today, I also do not eat after training. I stretch my fast through my morning surfing sessions and maintain fasting until lunch at around three o'clock p.m. and often even until dinner.

- Sauna – Just like extreme cold, extreme heat for at least 20 minutes can generate metabolic changes in the body that keep it healthy. Scandinavian studies have shown that continuous use of the sauna is associated with a longer life span. Infrared- and regular-heater saunas have many merits. Some, such as faster recovery and better detoxification through sweating, have special relevance for athletes. Sitting in a sauna also shifts gears from an intense, nervous, adrenaline-driven state to a more relaxed and healing supporting state. I have an infrared sauna at home, and I use it almost on a daily basis.

- Use of a foam roller – The foam roller is the professional and amateur athlete's best friend. A daily massage with a foam roller is vital. High-level professional athletes are attended by a team of masseurs who literally glue back together their connective tissues after being shattered in intensive contests or training. The foam roller is an acceptable substitute for those who cannot afford maintaining such a dedicated team at home.

- Food supplements – The sports world is filled with ability-boosting chemicals. From the enormous variety in existence, I choose only to recommend legal supplements, with solid research backing their effects, and with no side effects. Before an intensive skateboard session or challenging surfing, I use a combination of the following supplements: a medicinal mushroom cordyceps, Siberian ginseng, collagen or an essential amino-acids blend, and D-ribose powder. I also eat beets on a regular basis. All these have been scientifically proven to improve athletic capabilities. As I am also a Chinese medicine therapist, I am a great believer in medicinal herbs. That is why I take various combinations of low-dosage adaptogenic medicinal herbs daily, including ginseng, rhodiola, reishi, gynostemma and more. These herbs strengthen and vitalize our body and spirit. I also take collagen and vitamin C every day. Vitamin C is necessary for collagen synthesis, and since our connective tissue is composed of collagen, daily consumption of collagen accompanied by vitamin C is an excellent way of supporting and strengthening all components of the connective tissue – bones, tendons, the fascia, the disks, the ligaments and the skin.

CHAPTER 10

On the Dangers of Being Sedentary

The chairs we are sitting on, perhaps even at this very moment, entered the world at the time of the pharaohs. For thousands of years, the chair was no more than a prestigious item used exclusively by kings and noblemen. Commoners sat on the ground cross-legged, or they squatted or kneeled in a Japanese-like Seiza. At most, they would seat themselves on a random chest or a hard bench. In Europe during the Middle Ages, the chair grew increasingly popular and became a household item. It is, in fact, the most useful or at least the most-used human invention, perhaps even more than the wheel. Modern man first uses the chair around the age of one or two. Until then, the infant does just fine without it. In school, children will encounter the simple chair and sit on it for many long hours every day. Later on, at school and at work, the chair will become the most stable element of their lives. The evolution of the chair has made it particularly comfortable, with padding and extended surfaces, and new titles such as a couch or a sofa. Most of us spend the majority of our waking hours on this or that chair. The chair also fits in wonderfully with another invention – the table. And even better with a screen that glares in front of us. And this triad, which represents the current age – chair, table, computer – is quite simply killing us!

Studies have linked dozens of diseases and medical conditions with prolonged sitting, including cancer, heart diseases, depression, diabetes and even early mortality (Biswas et al., 2015; Schmid and Colditz, 2014; Chau et al., 2013; van der Ploeg, Chey, Korda, Banks & Bauman, 2012). Research has also shown that several hours of athletic activity a week cannot repair the damage caused by over one hundred hours of sitting a week. Our body knows how to sit, but it was never designed to sit. Sitting is simply not a position we were ever supposed to assume for as long as we do. It forces the body to shrink in on itself and collapse. Below are a few important and unfortunate facts that must be noted:

- The iliopsoas muscle, is one of the most important muscles in our body and it is hidden from view, embedded deep in our pelvis. This muscle supports a better posture of the lower spinal cord and helps the hip flex. This is the main muscle connecting our core to our feet. When we sit, the hip is constantly being passively bent, placing the iliopsoas in lax, and in time, causes it to weaken and become flabby. A weak iliopsoas makes our butt stick out. In professional doctor-speak, this situation is known as anterior tilt of the pelvis. The result is that our belly sticks out. An unstable pelvis and spine, together with a weak iliopsoas, are a definite recipe for lower back pain, disk ruptures, interruption of blood supply to the pelvis, knee pains and reduction in athletic capability. Furthermore, the iliopsoas is a classic survival muscle, for it enables us to run really quickly. When it passively lies there, sitting, it gradually weakens. Not good!
- The meaty buttocks muscles are not simply there to be sat upon. They are an important part of the muscle chain that is activated when we move, regardless of where and how. When we sit, these important muscles are completely switched off, and slowly disappear under a fatty layer that does a better and cheaper job of

comfortably supporting the upper body when we sit. This is not good and it does not look good, either!

- Our abdomen, with all its contents, undergoes serious compression when we sit. It is hard to believe that one can squeeze six meters (almost 20 feet) of digestive tract plus a few other organs into the narrow strip that is all that's left of the abdomen when we are seated and lean forward. When we sit, the abdominal organs are crushed together, and if that was not bad enough, our breathing becomes a shallow-chest breathing, for the diaphragm has no room to contract downwards. The entire blood flow and digestive process in the abdomen are impaired. Not good!

- Sitting leads to double chins. When we sit, our chins thrust forward, forming a rear arch in the neck. In other words, the posterior neck muscles contract and as a result, the anterior neck muscles, responsible for lowering the head and the chin, are lax. Just like the buttocks muscles. And just like the buttocks, over time this laxness clears the way for fat cells to grow in size with no competing muscle movement to oppose it. Half of our population lacks the ability to hide the double chin with a beard. So perhaps we should focus on prevention?

I could go on and on about the dangers of oversitting, but I don't want to be too depressing. So instead, I present to you several solutions I particularly like and implement daily:

- Get off the damn chair. Daily activity which is neither sitting nor physical training is also known as NEAT, or non-exercise thermogenesis. It was found that slim people have a higher NEAT. Additionally, they can intuitively raise it, and thereby burn off excess calories that they consume rather than gaining weight (Villablanca et al; 2015). That is why I simply recommend being as active as possible during the day, regardless of dedicated athletic activity. The idea is simple: minimum sitting and minimum standing still. You can count steps, though I find counting ten thousand steps a day to be arbitrary and unrealistic for most people, but it is better to simply take every opportunity to stand and move your body. While speaking on the phone, acquire the habit of walking or standing on one foot or squatting.

- Practice sitting, every day, in the positions we were designed for – particularly squatting and sitting cross-legged. Also, try to stand up and sit down without using your hands. A Brazilian study has found that individuals capable of sitting on the floor and standing up without using their hands, will live longer (Brito et al; 2014).
- Hanging and reverse hanging. If sitting is the "negative" of what our body was designed to do, an artificial and cramped posture, then hanging is the "positive" posture in which we reach maximal height and opening up of the chest and abdomen. I recommend scattering pull-up bars everywhere throughout your home. Reverse hanging is a bit complicated to practice on a daily basis and requires either very good athletic fitness or inversion boots or an inversion table.
- Massage your feet and hands. I constantly massage mine with small, thorny balls or a foot roller while working in the clinic. That way at least part of my body enjoys a massage.
- Try sitting in a chair without a backrest. In my clinic, I sit on a special knee-supportive chair that lacks a backrest. I recommend you look into ergonomic chairs and try to get used to a backrest-free chair. In the Alexander method, the recommended chair is a large physio ball. Its constant movements and instability turns sitting into a balance and core muscle exercise.
- Rebounding. This is the best way to increase the circulation of blood and lymph and to loosen up after prolonged stress.

To summarize, our incredible body is brilliantly constructed from a chain of hundreds of bones, joints and muscles, and is glued together into its configuration with a network and sleeves of fascia tissue and collagen fibers. All of these are intended for movement and motion. Our body is capable of much, much more than what we think it can do. Olympic runners prove what our bodies of capable of. It is a shame to limit all this beauty to cramped and sickly sitting for most of your life.

SOURCES

INTRODUCTION

1. U.S. Department of Health and Human Services. Public Health Service. Office of the Surgeon General. The Surgeon General's Vision for a Healthy and Fit Nation 2010.
2. Ofcom.org.uk. Children and Parents: Media Use and Attitudes Report.
3. Leatherdale S., Ahmed R. (2011). Screen-based sedentary be-haviours among a nationally representative sample of youth: are Canadian kids couch potatoes? *Chronic diseases and injuries in Canada*, 31, 141–146.

CHAPTER 1: THE PATTERN OF PHYSICAL ACTIVITY

1. Gillen JB, Martin BJ, MacInnis MJ, Skelly LE, Tarnopolsky MA, Gibala MJ (2016). Twelve Weeks of Sprint Interval Training Improves Indices of Cardiometabolic Health Similar to Traditional Endurance Training despite a Five-Fold Lower Exercise Volume and Time Commitment. PLoS ONE 11(4): e0154075. https://doi.org/10.1371/journal.pone.0154075
2. Gibala M, Shulgan C. The One-Minute Workout. 2017. Avery.

CHAPTER 3: SUPER-EXERCISES

1. Bhattacharya A, McCutcheon EP, Shvartz E, Greenleaf JE (1980). Body acceleration distribution and O2 uptake in humans during running and jumping. Journal of Applied Physiology, 49 (5): 881-887.
2. Bruney, J (2003). Neuro-Mass. The Ultimate System for Spectacular Strength. Dragon Door Publication, Inc.
3. Cugusi L, Manca A, Serpe R, Romita G, Bergamin M, Cadeddu C, Solla P, & Mercuro G (2016). Effects of a mini-trampoline rebounding exercise program on functional parameters, body composition and quality of life in overweight women. The Journal of Sports Medicine and Physical Fitness.
4. Yackle K, Schwarz LA, Kam K, Sorokin JM, Huguenard JR, Feldman JL, Luo L, & Krasnow MA (2017). Breathing control center neurons that promote arousal in mice. Science, 355(6332): 1411-1415. DOI: 10.1126/science.aai7984.

CHAPTER 4: MOVEMENT COMPONENT SPECIFIC SUPER-EXERCISES

1. Barbieri E, Agostin, D, Polidor, E, Potenza L, Guescini M, Lucertini F, Annibalini G, Stocchi L, De Santi M, & Stocchi V (2015). The pleiotropic effect of physical exercise on mitochondrial dynamics in aging skeletal muscle. Oxidative Medicine and Cellular Longevity, 917085. doi: 10.1155/2015/917085. https://www.ncbi.nlm.nih.gov/pubmed/25945152
2. Carter HN, Chen CC, & Hood DA (2015). Mitochondria, muscle health, and exercise with advancing age. Physiology (Bethesda). 30(3):208-23. doi: 10.1152/physiol.00039.2014. https://www.ncbi.nlm.nih.gov/pubmed/25933821

3. Johnson LM, Robinson MM, & Nair KS (2013). Skeletal muscle aging and the mitochondria. Trends in Endocrinology & Metabolism, 24(5): 247–256. https://www.ncbi.nlm.nih.gov/pmc/articles/PMC3641176/

CHAPTER 6: SUPER-EXERCISE TRAINING IN ILLNESS

1. Physical Activity Guidelines for Americans, by the Office of Disease Prevention & Health Promotion, 2008, U.S. Department of Health and Human Services. http://www.health.gov/PAGuidelines/default.aspx

CHAPTER 7: FASCIA? WHAT IS THAT?

1. Hoffrén-Mikkola M, Ishikawa M, Rantalainen T, Avela J, Komi PV. (2015). Neuromuscular mechanics and hopping training in elderly. European Journal of Applied Physiology, 115(5):863-77. doi: 10.1007/s00421-014-3065-9. Epub 2014 Dec.

CHAPTER 8: MOTIVATION, FLOW, POTENTIAL

1. Reasons for Participating in a Serious Leisure Career: Comparison of Canadian and U.S. -Masters Swimmers. Donald W. Hastings, Suzanne B. Kurth, Monika Schloder. International Review for the Sociology of Sport.
2. Ogles BM, Masters KS, Richardson SA (1995). Obligatory running and gender: An-analysis of participative motives and training habits. International Journal of Sport Psychology, 26, 233–248.
3. Performance Discourses and Old Age: What Does It Mean to Be an Older Athlete. Rylee Dionigi, Gabrielle O'Flynn. DEC 2007 SOCIOLOGY OF SPORT JOURNAL.

CHAPTER 10: ON THE DANGERS OF BEING SEDENTARY

1. Biswas A, Oh PI, Faulkner GE, Bajaj RR, Silver MA, Mitchell MS, et al. (2015). Sedentary time and its association with risk for disease incidence, mortality, and hospitalization in adults: a systematic review and meta-analysis. Annals of Internal Medicine, 162, 123–132. doi: 10.7326/M14-1651.
2. Brito LB, Ricardo DR, Araújo DS, Ramos PS, Myers J, and Araújo CG (2014). Ability to sit and rise from the floor as a predictor of all-cause mortality. European Journal of Preventive Cardiology, 21(7):892-8. doi: 10.1177/2047487312471759. Epub 2012 Dec 13.
3. Chau JY, Grunseit AC, Chey T, Stamatakis E, Brown WJ, Matthews CE, et al. (2013). Daily sitting time and all-cause mortality: A meta-analysis. PLoS ONE 8:e80000. doi: 10.1371/ journal.pone.0080000.
4. Schmid D, and Leitzmann MF (2014). Television Viewing and Time Spent Sedentary in Relation to Cancer Risk: A Meta-analysis. JNCI Journal of the National Cancer Institute, 106 (7): dju098 DOI: 10.1093/jnci/dju098.
5. Van der Ploeg HP, Chey T, Korda RJ, Banks E, and Bauman A (2012). Sitting time and all-cause mortality risk in 222 497 Australian adults. Archives of internal medicine 172 (6), 494-500.
6. Villablanca PA, Alegria JR, Mookadam F, Holmes Jr DR, Wright RS, Levine JA (2015). Nonexercise Activity Thermogenesis in